The Last of the Mohicans is the most widely rea
claimed of James Fenimore Cooper's Leatherstoc
tionally been regarded as an exciting and well-
recent years, however, critics have found in th
warfare deeper levels of meaning. In the introdu
Daniel Peck studies these developments, tracking critical responses to the
novel from the time of its publication in 1826 to the present day.

The essays that follow present contemporary reassessments of *The Last
of the Mohicans* from a variety of critical perspectives. Wayne Franklin
shows how Cooper's depiction of Glens Falls – the site of one of the
novel's key scenes – represents the process by which the writer dreams his
way into the American past. Terence Martin examines the novel's great
pivotal episode, the massacre at Fort William Henry, revealing how this
specifically historical event marginalizes and displaces even the heroic
Uncas and Natty Bumppo, thus replicating the very force of history. Nina
Baym positions the novel, critically, between the works of two women
writers of the 1820s, Lydia Maria Child and Catherine Maria Sedgwick,
showing how their women-centered narratives implicitly challenge
Cooper's assumptions about sexual, racial, and social roles. Shirley Samuels, combining feminist and new historicist approaches, considers the
theme of cultural miscegenation and demonstrates how the novel's pervasive confusions of identity dramatize an intense fear of women and of
natural reproduction. Finally, Robert Lawson-Peebles shows how the carnage of the massacre of Fort William Henry may be understood as a
violation of European theories of warfare, and how this violation reveals
Cooper's attitudes toward the New World environment.

NEW ESSAYS ON THE LAST OF THE MOHICANS

★ The American Novel ★

GENERAL EDITOR
Emory Elliott
University of California, Riverside

Other books in the series:
New Essays on The Scarlet Letter
New Essays on The Great Gatsby
New Essays on Adventures of Huckleberry Finn
New Essays on Moby-Dick
New Essays on Uncle Tom's Cabin
New Essays on The Red Badge of Courage
New Essays on The Sun Also Rises
New Essays on A Farewell to Arms
New Essays on The American
New Essays on The Portrait of a Lady
New Essays on Light in August
New Essays on The Awakening
New Essays on Invisible Man
New Essays on Native Son
New Essays on Their Eyes Were Watching God
New Essays on The Grapes of Wrath
New Essays on Winesburg, Ohio
New Essays on Sister Carrie
New Essays on The Rise of Silas Lapham
New Essays on The Catcher in the Rye
New Essays on White Noise
New Essays on The Crying of Lot 49

New Essays on
The Last of the Mohicans

Edited by
H. Daniel Peck

Published by the Press Syndicate of the University of Cambridge
The Pitt Building, Trumpington Street, Cambridge CB2 1RP
40 West 20th Street, New York, NY 10011-4211, USA
10 Stamford Road, Oakleigh, Victoria 3166, Australia

First published 1992

Printed in the United States of America

Library of Congress Cataloging-in-Publication Data

New essays on the last of the Mohicans / edited by H. Daniel Peck.
        p.   cm. – (The American novel)
    ISBN 0-521-37414-6 – ISBN 0-521-37771-4
1. Cooper, James Fenimore, 1789–1851. Last of the Mohicans.
2. United States – History – French and Indian War, 1755–1763 –
    Literature and the war.   3. Mohegan Indians in literature.
            I. Peck, H. Daniel.   II. Series.
                PS1408.N48   1992
            813'.2 – dc20   91-33425

A catalog record for this book is available from the British Library.

            ISBN 0-521-37414-6   hardback
            ISBN 0-521-37771-4   paperback

Contents

Series Editor's Preface
page vii

1
Introduction
H. DANIEL PECK
page 1

2
The Wilderness of Words in
The Last of the Mohicans
WAYNE FRANKLIN
page 25

3
From Atrocity to Requiem: History in
The Last of the Mohicans
TERENCE MARTIN
page 47

4
How Men and Women Wrote Indian Stories
NINA BAYM
page 67

Contents

5

Generation through Violence: Cooper
and the Making of Americans
SHIRLEY SAMUELS
page 87

6

The Lesson of the Massacre
at Fort William Henry
ROBERT LAWSON-PEEBLES
page 115

Notes on Contributors
page 139

Selected Bibliography
page 141

Series Editor's Preface

In literary criticism the last twenty-five years have been particularly fruitful. Since the rise of the New Criticism in the 1950s, which focused attention of critics and readers upon the text itself – apart from history, biography, and society – there has emerged a wide variety of critical methods which have brought to literary works a rich diversity of perspectives: social, historical, political, psychological, economic, ideological, and philosophical. While attention to the text itself, as taught by the New Critics, remains at the core of contemporary interpretation, the widely shared assumption that works of art generate many different kinds of interpretation has opened up possibilities for new readings and new meanings.

Before this critical revolution, many American novels had come to be taken for granted by earlier generations of readers as having an established set of recognized interpretations. There was a sense among many students that the canon was established and that the larger thematic and interpretative issues had been decided. The task of the new reader was to examine the ways in which elements such as structure, style, and imagery contributed to each novel's acknowledged purpose. But recent criticism has brought these old assumptions into question and has thereby generated a wide variety of original, and often quite surprising, interpretations of the classics, as well as of rediscovered novels such as Kate Chopin's *The Awakening*, which has only recently entered the canon of works that scholars and critics study and that teachers assign their students.

The aim of The American Novel Series is to provide students of American literature and culture with introductory critical guides to

American novels now widely read and studied. Each volume is devoted to a single novel and begins with an introduction by the volume editor, a distinguished authority on the text. The introduction presents details of the novel's composition, publication history, and contemporary reception, as well as a survey of the major critical trends and readings from first publication to the present. This overview is followed by four or five original essays, specifically commissioned from senior scholars of established reputation and from outstanding younger critics. Each essay presents a distinct point of view, and together they constitute a forum of interpretative methods and of the best contemporary ideas on each text.

It is our hope that these volumes will convey the vitality of current critical work in American literature, generate new insights and excitement for students of the American novel, and inspire new respect for and new perspectives upon these major literary texts.

Emory Elliott
University of California, Riverside

1

Introduction

H. DANIEL PECK

*T*HE *Last of the Mohicans* is a pivotal work in James Fenimore Cooper's first, remarkable decade of authorship, the 1820s, and in his career as a whole. This was his sixth novel, published in 1826, and its setting and themes are anticipated by several of the works that precede it. Following his first book, an unsuccessful novel of manners called *Precaution* (1820), Cooper found his form, materials, and indeed, his audience, with *The Spy* (1821), a tale of the American Revolution set in the rocky highlands above colonial New York City. Like Washington Irving's work of the same period, this novel demonstrated that American settings and history (George Washington figures in the novel's action) could be made to serve fiction. Although this novel's paradigms of character, plot, and setting derived from Sir Walter Scott ("the American Scott" is an appellation Cooper never liked, and did not outlive), Cooper filled the paradigms with his own distinctive elements.

Most important, he adapted Scott's setting of the "neutral ground," a disputed territory contested by two or more warring parties, to the American landscape. In *The Spy*, this landscape is characterized by a ruggedness that obscures human lines of demarcation and often defeats the attempts of the characters to command its difficult terrain. Out of this setting is born a hero whose uncanny ability to successfully negotiate the landscape defines his heroism. Harvey Birch, a counterspy serving the American forces, is Cooper's first great mythic character. In this figure of daring, skill, and perceptual acuity, Cooper created the model for his Leatherstocking hero.

The Leatherstocking hero, however, as he first emerged in Cooper's fiction, is hardly the equal of Harvey Birch. In *The Pi-*

1

oneers, the writer's third novel, published in 1823, Natty Bumppo is an aged woodsman living near Templeton, a frontier settlement drawn from Cooper's childhood memories of Cooperstown. With his Indian companion Chingachgook (known as Indian John in this novel), Natty Bumppo serves primarily to remind the community of its "wasty ways," its mindless destruction of the natural environment; he represents a commitment to the wilderness which, the novel makes clear, is increasingly difficult to honor. Indeed, Natty's departure for the West at the novel's conclusion suggests the inevitability of change and the irrevocable nature of American "progress." The Leatherstocking of *The Pioneers,* essentially powerless before the emerging forces of civilization (his imprisonment in the stocks symbolizes this), is, in several ways, a marginal figure, one of the several frontier "characters" in the novel whose time has come and gone.

When Cooper took up the Leatherstocking figure again in *The Last of the Mohicans* three years later, removing his setting to the French and Indian War of the mid-eighteenth century, he returned him to vigorous middle age and gave him back the powers which had ebbed in *The Pioneers.* Contributing largely to the significance of *The Last of the Mohicans* is the emergence of the Leatherstocking as a fully realized frontier hero − the model for countless imitations in the nineteenth and twentieth centuries. Adding further significance is that, in writing the novel, Cooper began to consider his hero as part of an ongoing series, a saga of frontier life in America.

Before he came to *The Last of the Mohicans,* however, Cooper published two other novels: *The Pilot* (1824), a highly successful tale of the sea, pitting American and British naval forces against one another during the Revolution, and *Lionel Lincoln* (1825), a story of revolutionary Boston whose mixture of gothicism and historical romance worked to ill effect. Despite their different degrees of success and different settings, however, both works presage *The Last of the Mohicans.*

The rugged and fog-shrouded shoreline of *The Pilot*'s English coastline, a further development of the disputed neutral ground, anticipates the dangerous, war-torn landscape of *The Last of the Mohicans.* The selfless courage of the seaman Tom Coffin suggests

2

the simple nobility of Natty Bumppo, and the perceptual acuity of the novel's Byronic hero, John Paul Jones, anticipates the Leatherstocking's uncanny ability to successfully negotiate a setting of violence and conflict. In *Lionel Lincoln*, Cooper took the neutral ground to its most extreme limits, depicting a landscape so dangerously obscure that it becomes, in several of its key scenes, a world of nightmare. His rendering of the Battle of Bunker Hill prefigures, in its violence and confusion, the Massacre at Fort William Henry in *The Last of the Mohicans*.

By the time Cooper published *The Last of the Mohicans* in early February of 1826, he was already a celebrity in American literary circles. *The Spy, The Pioneers,* and *The Pilot* had been best-sellers and the immediate and extraordinary success of *The Last of the Mohicans* confirmed his reputation as the leading American novelist of his generation. When on June 1, 1826, four months after the book's publication, Cooper departed with his family for an extended European sojourn, he was a national hero. At this point, the next Leatherstocking tale was already under way; *The Prairie* was completed in Europe and published in 1827. Here Cooper took the aged hero of *The Pioneers* to an even more advanced age and to America's far West. In *The Prairie,* Natty Bumppo refers to events and characters from both *The Pioneers* and *The Last of the Mohicans;* in several ways the novel recapitulates themes and ideas treated in the earlier works. With Natty's death at the conclusion of *The Prairie* came the end of the Leatherstocking saga, or so Cooper thought at the time.

Cooper spent seven years in Europe, returning home in 1833, and during his time away the nation's affection for him waned. His involvement in European political affairs, particularly the so-called Finance Controversy, had made him unpopular at home; and the novels treating the European past that he had written while abroad (*The Bravo* [1831], *The Heidenmauer* [1832], and *The Headsman* [1833]) were not popular, although these works implicitly celebrated American democracy by depicting Europe's dark, feudal past. Misunderstood and, in his opinion, unappreciated, Cooper returned to his homeland in a state of disaffection from which he never recovered.

The 1830s were marked by Cooper's further alienation from his native land. The full emergence of Jacksonian democracy brought with it leveling tendencies that threatened the landed gentry on whom America, in Cooper's view, depended for political and cultural leadership. Everywhere he looked, he saw narrow self-interest, greed, and a general breakdown of decorum in social life. Cooper's novel of 1838, *Home as Found*, dramatized this threat. In this work, the descendants of *The Pioneers'* Oliver and Elizabeth Effingham had become a beleaguered minority, struggling to defend their very survival as a class. That the novel dramatizes an actual event from Cooper's life during the 1830s – an attempt to reclaim his family's ownership of a public picnic area near Cooperstown – confirms that his sense of threat to America's gentry was deeply personal. Other work of this period, such as his allegorical novel, *The Monikins* (1835), has a strongly polemical quality, reflecting Cooper's dominant political and social concerns during the 1830s.

Then, in 1840, perhaps out of a need to retreat from the pressing difficulties of his public life (including a series of libel suits he brought against newspapers in this period) and also to recover his flagging reputation as a novelist, Cooper returned to the Leatherstocking series and to the genre that had made him famous, the historical romance. He brought Natty Bumppo back to life in *The Pathfinder*, set on and around Lake Ontario where Cooper himself had served in the U.S. Navy during his young manhood. Roughly the same age as he was in *The Last of the Mohicans*, Natty Bumppo is here characterized in softer terms. No longer the hard-hearted scout committed only to his duty, his "gifts," and his Indian companions, he falls in love. In this novel, Cooper explored the possibility of reconciling an ethos of wilderness adventure with one of domesticity. That the Leatherstocking fails to win the heroine, Mabel Dunham, and returns to the forest with his Indian companion Chingachgook suggests the impossibility in Cooper's mind of such a reconciliation.

The following year Cooper published *The Deerslayer*, taking his hero back to his youthful initiation into wilderness adventure. The setting, Lake Otsego (called the Glimmerglass in this novel), is the same as in the first-written of the Leatherstocking tales, *The Pioneers*, but in a period half a century earlier and predating white

4

settlement. The historical remoteness and the wilderness setting, as well as the hero's youth, make *The Deerslayer* the most romantic of the Leatherstocking tales, and suggest the writer's need to re-possess imaginatively a simpler world associated with his child-hood in Cooperstown. With this novel, the Leatherstocking series was complete; in the hero's beginning was his end.

Cooper's prolific career continued for another decade, during which he published a number of important works, including the Littlepage trilogy (1845–46), a series of novels dramatizing the dispossession of the landed gentry in New York State during the Anti-Rent Wars, and *The Crater* (1847), a novel allegorizing the rise and fall of the United States. At the end of his life, however, Cooper himself knew that the Leatherstocking tales were the works for which he would be best remembered. What he may not have fully understood is the special place within the tales that *The Last of the Mohicans* would forever hold.

The immediate impetus for writing *The Last of the Mohicans* seems to have been a sight-seeing tour of the Hudson River that Cooper made with a group of young British noblemen during the autumn of 1824, encompassing West Point, Albany, Saratoga, and Ballston. Standing in the caverns at the picturesque Glens Falls, one of the British tourists, Edward Stanley, made a remark that Cooper seems to have taken as a challenge: "Here is the very scene for a ro-mance." After the novel was published, Cooper saw to it that Stanley received a copy.[1]

If the novel grew, in part, from such a challenge, it would not have been uncharacteristic of Cooper. His imagination is primarily visual, and he responded deeply to the scenic aspects of landscape. For example, Susan Fenimore Cooper said that a sudden glimpse of Lake Otsego through the forest inspired her father to begin writing *The Deerslayer*.[2]

While the scene of Glens Falls may have served Cooper as the initial impetus for writing *The Last of the Mohicans*, the narrative and symbolic meanings he invested in this site, and in the novel's larger geography as well, came from his own interior landscape. That landscape, in all its rich complexity, has been the subject of much recent critical commentary, which has recognized *The Last of the Mohicans* as a key representation of the novelist's deepest personal and historical concerns. As Wayne Franklin points out in the present collection, Cooper's appropriation of Glens Falls, the setting for one of the novel's most riveting scenes, "depended on radical erasures." It involved Cooper's dreaming his way backward from the deteriorated falls and tourist structures he found at the site in 1824 to a true wilderness setting. The erasure and reconfiguration of the landscape, as Franklin shows, are among the deepest sources of Cooper's power as a novelist in *The Last of the Mohicans,* and in his other fiction as well.

In his first preface to *The Last of the Mohicans,* however, Cooper went out of his way to discourage such symbolic interpretations. This book, he said, was simply a "narrative," and he instructed readers not to seek within it "an imaginary and romantic picture of things" (p. 1). In doing this, Cooper was, in part, warning readers of refined taste, especially "young ladies" (p. 4), away from a work in which he had attempted to draw vividly some of the bloodiest scenes in American colonial history. His testimony regarding accurate representation, especially concerning American Indian tribes and their allegiances, is the singular focus of this first preface.[3]

Cooper's representations of history and Indian life (this was the first novel in which he had undertaken to treat Indians extensively) came under immediate attack in some contemporary reviews. A review in the May 1826 issue of the *London Magazine* referred to *The Last of the Mohicans* as "clearly by much the worst of Mr. Cooper's performances," and drew attention to the "[i]mprobabilities" of its action and characterizations. The American critic W. H. Gardiner was far more sympathetic in his treatment of the novel, but one of his criticisms was that it followed too faithfully the "wild traditions" of the missionary John Heckewelder. These, Gardiner argued, had led Cooper to present "altogether a false and ideal view of the Indian character." "We should be glad to know," he asked, "in what tribe, or in what age of Indian history, such a civilized warrior as Uncas ever flourished?"[4]

A similar attack came from a presumed authority, General Lewis Cass, an Indian fighter and agent, who, in 1828 said that Uncas has "no living prototype in our forests." Attacks such as these continued in the years following the publication of *The Last of the Mohicans,* and in 1835 the Philadelphia writer and dramatist William Bird published a novel, *Nick of the Woods,* intended, he said later, to debunk what he regarded as Cooper's idealized characterizations of Indians in *The Last of the Mohicans.* Even Francis Parkman, in his generally admiring survey of Cooper's works written soon after the novelist's death in 1852, said that Cooper's "Indian characters . . . it must be granted, are for the most part either superficially or falsely drawn."[5]

None of this diminished the novel's popularity with the reading public; for an entire century after its publication, it remained the most internationally acclaimed and widely translated of Cooper's works. Professional literary appraisals, however, continued throughout most of the nineteenth century to emphasize the ideality of Cooper's characterizations, and regularly caricatured his treatment of the Indians. Mark Twain's famous essay, "Fenimore Cooper's Literary Offenses," is merely the most ingenious in a long series of attacks on the credibility of Cooper's representations.

Both Cooper and *The Last of the Mohicans* did have their notable defenders during this period. The American novelist William Gilmore Simms, whose *The Yemassee* (1835) may be considered a counterpart to *The Last of the Mohicans* in its mournful treatment of Indian dispossession in the South, praised Cooper for his "[inimitable] details of Indian art and resource." Honoré de Balzac, in his warm appreciation of Cooper published in 1840, ranked *The Last of the Mohicans* among the seven works of the novelist which he said "are his unique and rightful claim to fame."[6]

The first fully analytical attempts to rescue Cooper, and *The Last of the Mohicans,* from caricature had to await the early twentieth century. W. C. Brownell's perceptive essay on Cooper in his 1909 *American Prose Masters* is the most important of such efforts. In acknowledging that the "verisimilitude of Cooper's Indians has been the main point of attack of his caricaturing critics," Brownell countered, "it is the fact that the so-called 'noble red man,' whom he is popularly supposed to have invented, does not exist in his books at all. Successful or not, his Indians, like his other characters, belong to the realm of attempted portraiture of racial types, and are, in intention, at all events, in no wise purely romantic creations." Cooper's Indian characters, Brownell continued, "are as carefully studied and as successfully portrayed as his white ones. . . . They are as much personalities and differ from each other as much." Later in the twentieth century, a European scholar recognized the degree to which Cooper's Indians are related to certain ideal types such as Scott's clan chieftains, Byron's pirates, and Ossian's Celtic heroes – that they are indeed ideal types, but in a recognizably romantic sense that belongs to the age in which they were written.[7]

In our own time, Cooper's representation of Indians has come under a new form of attack, against which Brownell's defense (essentially aesthetic in character) seems hardly adequate. Revisionist literary historians do not accept Brownell's assumption that "fiction is, to some extent, at least, outside [ethnology's] jurisdiction."[8] They demonstrate the ways in which Cooper's characterizations of Indians, no matter how distinguishable one Indian "type" is from another in his fiction, belong to the larger racial stereotypes that pervaded American thought in the nineteenth century. One such critic, specifically considering *The Last of the Mohicans,* writes: "We may even say that Cooper never loves his Indians so much as when he is watching them disappear, and that for him as for General Sheridan – although with a different emphasis – the only good Indians were dead."[9] That Cooper's mournful treatment of Indian dispossession is, at heart, a sentimental response covertly justifying that very dispossession is a steadily articulated theme in contemporary criticism.[10]

Other scholars in our time have come to Cooper's defense in this matter, by placing his work in historical perspective. James F. Beard, for example, introduces *The Last of the Mohicans* in the following way: "Though Cooper seems never to have prepared a systematic list of readings, the extraordinary assimilation of information displayed in his fiction suggests that his knowledge of Indians was as full and authentic as discriminating study of the printed sources of his time allowed." Beard shows that Cooper went out of his way to meet and interview several of the great Indian chiefs of his day, and that, unlike most Americans of his generation, he was skeptical about the policy of Indian Removal that began with the 1823 Supreme Court decision denying that the Indians' "right of discovery" was a sufficient legal basis for land ownership.[11]

Further, some critics of our time have recognized in *The Last of the Mohicans*, and in others of Cooper's Indian novels, a genuinely felt sense of loss, and even a deep personal identification with Indian dispossession. It is noteworthy that in the years immediately before Cooper wrote *The Last of the Mohicans*, he was dispossessed of vast lands in central New York left to him and his brothers by their land-baron father, William Cooper. The Indians' original ownership of the land is a central point of *The Pioneers*, published three years before *The Last of the Mohicans*. Cooper's sense of threatened class and power, characteristic of him throughout his career, informs all his fiction and repeatedly makes possession the central issue of his novels, whether set in the wilderness, at sea, or in society. The psychic union of Indian dispossession and Cooper's own threatened losses has been posited by several modern commentators, and has been offered as an explanation for the power of Cooper's elegiac vision in *The Last of the Mohicans*.[12]

Certainly it is true that no white American writer of the early and middle nineteenth century (not even Thoreau, as Robert F. Sayre has shown[13]) was free of racial prejudice toward Indians, and, in the end, an exception cannot be made of Cooper. Yet, while rigorously analyzing racial attitudes in his fiction as a means of understanding the racism of our society, we need to be equally rigorous in developing the historical context surrounding Cooper's work. We also need to read the novels more carefully. Close scrutiny of *The Last of the Mohicans* tells us, for example, that Cooper never undercuts the claims of his "bad" Indian Magua, who argues that his deep malevolence proceeds from degradation at the hands of European military forces and from white "gluttony." Furthermore, it is given over to Magua, through his "artful eloquence" (p. 175), to express the novel's most compelling elegiac vision of Indian dispossession:

[The white man's] gluttony makes him sick. God gave him enough, and yet he wants all. Such are the pale faces.
Some the Great Spirit made with skins brighter and redder than yonder sun, . . . and these did he fashion to his own mind. He gave

them this island as he had made it, covered with trees, and filled with game. The wind made their clearings; the sun and rains ripened their fruits; and the snows came to tell them to be thankful. What need had they of roads to journey by! They saw through the hills. (p. 301)

In several respects, Magua is the most fully and successfully delineated character in *The Last of the Mohicans*, rising above stereotypes of the bad Indian. On the one hand, his motives and feelings are rendered with focused particularity (unlike those of the more abstracted and idealized Uncas). On the other hand, his stature, especially in the second half of the novel, rises to that of legendary malignancy; he becomes "the Prince of Darkness" (p. 284).

If Cooper's instruction to read *The Last of the Mohicans* as a "narrative" failed to persuade critics intent upon faulting his representation of Indians, in another respect it succeeded better than he could have known. For the word "narrative," as Cooper uses it in his preface, means not only fidelity to fact but also efficacy of plot. To a large degree, critics and general readers from his own time through at least the middle of the twentieth century have viewed the novel primarily as a "narrative" in just this sense – as a well made, fast-moving, and exciting tale of adventure. An early (unsigned) review, published in the *New York Review and Atheneum* in March of 1826, shortly after the novel's publication, is an example: "[W]e are carried onward, as through the visions of a long and feverish dream. The excitement cannot be controlled or lulled, by which we are borne through strange and fearful, and even agonizing scenes of doubt, surprise, danger, and sudden deliverance." W. H. Gardiner, in the review cited earlier, praised the novel for the "intense and breathless interest" of its story.[14]

Cooper's biographer of the late nineteenth century, Thomas R. Lounsbury, said that *The Last of the Mohicans* "is the one [novel in Cooper's canon] in which the interest not only never halts, but never sinks." For Lounsbury, the novel's "improbability of action, insufficiency of motive, and feebleness of outline in many of the leading characters" were but "minor drawbacks" which, set against its driving, powerful narrative, "sink into absolute insignificance." The continuity of this response deep into the twentieth century is evidenced in an influential critical biography by James Grossman published in 1949. According to Grossman, *The Last of the Mohicans* is a "'pure' adventure story" that "has no serious concern with the outside world which it uses as a decoration and an aid to the action."[15] Such testimony is compelling in part because it is so widespread. Readers from Cooper's own land and from around the world have consistently ranked *The Last of the Mohicans* as his most exciting wilderness tale. That both Hollywood and the British Broadcasting Corporation have translated the novel to film (the latter with great effectiveness) is further testimony to the excitement generated by its breathless pacing.

The narrative development of *The Last of the Mohicans* is one of few aspects of the novel that most critics, both past and present, have agreed to praise. Compared to *The Deerslayer,* a hundred pages longer and filled with seemingly interminable passages of inert dialogue (it was *The Deerslayer* on which Twain focused his scorn), it stands forth as *the* distinctive example of how good a storyteller Cooper can be, how well he can turn characterization and setting into overriding imperatives of action. Yet a century of such praise has had some unfortunate effects. It has tended to obscure the ways in which *The Last of the Mohicans* makes claims on our imaginations that transcend its strictly "narrative" elements.

One of the first readers to acknowledge these claims, and one of the most influential of all Cooper's critics, was D. H. Lawrence. In his brilliant essay on the Leatherstocking tales, first published in the *English Review* and later collected in *Studies in Classic American Literature* (1923), Lawrence found in Cooper a deeply divided sensibility, one part of him longing for wilderness freedom and the other begging for recognition from the civilized, European world of letters.

According to Lawrence, the tension in Cooper between "Wish Fulfillment" and "Actuality" resulted in a pervasive "duplicity" which, once understood, revealed a deeply mythic level of meaning in the Leatherstocking tales. The tales, in this view, "go backwards, from old age to golden youth. That is the true myth of America. She starts old, wrinkled and writhing in the old skin. And there is a gradual sloughing of the old skin, towards a new

11

youth. It is the myth of America." This myth was founded, Lawrence said, on a "new relationship" that promised a "new society": "a stark, stripped human relationship of two men [Leatherstocking and Chingachgook], deeper than the deeps of sex." For Lawrence, this new relationship was central to *The Last of the Mohicans:* "Beyond all this heart-beating" – the novel's romantic triangle of Uncas, Cora, and Magua, as well as the romance between Duncan Heyward and Alice Munro – "stands the figures of Natty and Chingachgook: the two childless, womanless men, of opposite races. They are the abiding . . . [and represent] the inception of a new humanity."[16]

All the major strains of Cooper criticism that emerged in the 1950s and 1960s – primarily under the impetus of the so-called myth and symbol school of American studies – are indebted to Lawrence's insights. This is true, for example, of the interpretation of R. W. B. Lewis, who saw Leatherstocking as an archetypal American "hero in space," born out of the mythic possibilities of the American landscape. With their heavily conceptual emphases, interpretations of *The Last of the Mohicans* written in this period tended to place the novel within mythopoetic and historical patterns belonging to the Leatherstocking tales as a whole, rather than considering the novel on its own terms. Consider, for example, Henry Nash Smith's reading of the tales as a dramatization of "the problem of social order." For Joel Porte, the tales, including *The Last of the Mohicans,* exemplified a unique form of American "romance," while for Roy Harvey Pearce and Edwin Fussell they exemplified American attitudes toward the frontier.[17]

The most influential of mythic interpretations from this period, however, and the one most directly derived from Lawrence's insights, is Leslie Fiedler's. Fiedler found in the novel's pervasive doubling of characters and plots (its light and dark heroines, "good" and "bad" Indians, and two distinct journeys) a reflection of the novelist's "ambivalence toward the instinctual life in sex and nature." For Fiedler, the "secret theme" of *The Last of the Mohicans* is miscegenation, Cooper's horror of which "led him to forbid even the not-quite white offspring [Cora Munro] of one unnatural marriage to enter into another alliance [with Uncas] that crossed race lines." According to this view, Cooper's only recourse in formulating the possibilities for race relations in America was to posit a sexless – though nascently homoerotic – love between the Leatherstocking and Chingachgook. For Fiedler, then, here was the (Freudian) core of the "new relationship" that Lawrence had discovered in the Leatherstocking tales.[18]

In the 1960s a number of critics challenged Fiedler's formulation. George Dekker made the point in 1967 that the theme of miscegenation in *The Last of the Mohicans* – and in others of Cooper's works such as *The Wept of Wish-ton-Wish* (1829) – is hardly secret. Following the emphasis given earlier by Donald Davie, Dekker reminded us that Cooper's characters, like Scott's, always represent national, regional, and social classes: "An experienced reader of Cooper should therefore guess at once that when mulatto Cora and Indian Uncas are attracted to each other, Cooper is dealing with the relations between the three main races then inhabiting North America, and testing the possibility of their being brought together. It is the sort of subject in which Cooper was characteristically interested, and the method he employs is equally characteristic."[19]

Dekker's challenge to Fiedler is essentially the challenge of the historian to the mythic critic, and it is certainly true that mythic criticism of the 1950s and 1960s, in viewing the Leatherstocking tales as a conceptual whole, largely ignored a central historical fact: The five tales were written over a period of eighteen years, and reflect a number of significant changes of emphasis and, indeed, some major discontinuities. In 1971, Thomas Philbrick focused this point on *The Last of the Mohicans*, emphasizing the novel's disconnection from the other tales. Philbrick argued that a close reading of *The Last of the Mohicans* revealed a world so full of discord (the rushing waters at Glens, falling "by no rule at all" [p. 55], symbolized this world) that the novel could not be said to be "about" anything at all, unless it were chaos itself. Attempts to find meaning and significant narrative patterns in this "landscape of nightmare," Philbrick argued, were pointless because they ask questions of the novel which are "inappropriate and hence incapable of yielding conclusive answers . . . [because they] presuppose the existence of conscious intellectual control by the novelist over the materials of his fiction and assume that those materials are ordered in an ideological scheme which, once identified, will unlock the meaning of the book."[20]

Philbrick's essay was a key development in the history of criticism of *The Last of the Mohicans.* In its close examination of the text it made impossible, henceforth, any easy application of myth and symbol formulations to the novel. It was unsatisfying, however, as a full interpretation because it so completely divorced *The Last of the Mohicans* from the body of Cooper's fiction, almost as if Cooper hadn't written it (Philbrick argued that a feverish case of sunstroke Cooper suffered during the composition of the novel helps account for its anomalous features). In arguing that the book is "profoundly different in nature from Cooper's other fiction,"[21] he offered no way in which to consider its relation to that other fiction.

In providing so close an examination of the novel's language and imagery, however, Philbrick implicitly challenged critics to seek new bases on which to ground its relation to the other Leatherstocking tales, and to Cooper's fiction as a whole. During the 1970s, a number of critics took up this challenge. In my own 1977 study of Cooper, for example, I attempt to tie *The Last of the Mohicans* to the body of Cooper's fiction by viewing it as a climactic representation of a "landscape of difficulty" characteristic of all Cooper's early novels; such landscapes, I argue, objectify deeply felt issues of dispossession that come to a focus in this work. Stephen Railton, in a 1978 psychoanalytic study of Cooper, finds in one of the novel's most visually turbulent moments – a scene of furious hand-to-hand combat between Chingachgook and Magua – representation of a severe oedipal struggle in the writer, a struggle he finds generative in Cooper's work as a whole. In a 1982 study of Cooper's settlement novels, Wayne Franklin views *The Last of the Mohicans* as "the most private of Cooper's fictions"; unlike settlement novels such as *The Pioneers,* he argues, it licenses the writer's "delight in disorder" and thereby reveals an anarchic aspect of Cooper's sensibility largely masked, but nevertheless present, in his other works.[22]

If Cooper criticism of the late 1970s and early 1980s was characterized by probes into the writer's interior landscape, the period since that time has returned us to historical and cultural concerns, though with different emphases from the mythopoetic readings of the 1950s and 1960s, and from still earlier historical treatments such as those by Vernon L. Parrington and Robert E. Spiller in the 1920s and 1930s. These new interpretations have been influenced by poststructuralist theory, including deconstruction, and most recently by the new historicism. (Structuralist criticism of the 1960s and early 1970s, such as that inspired by the anthropologist Claude Lévi-Strauss, had little direct impact on Cooper studies – a curious fact, given that novels like *The Last of the Mohicans* present complex issues of social organization and portrayals of ritual.[23]) William P. Kelly's 1983 study of the Leatherstocking tales is the first book to fully reflect these new approaches. Kelly sees in the tales Cooper's struggle to reconcile American adamism and an opposing cultural myth of historical entailment. In this view, *The Last of the Mohicans* is a pivotal work reflecting Cooper's deeply ambivalent responses to history; the wholesale destruction of the massacre of Fort William Henry, Kelly argues, prepares the possibility for America's full cultural originality, but the novel's cyclical structure asserts historical continuity.[24]

Although Kelly's book is the first to treat the historical dimension of *The Last of the Mohicans* through a generally deconstructive analysis, the idea that history is at the center of the novel's meaning – and that the massacre of Fort William Henry is the nexus of this meaning – has been with us for several decades. Terence Martin recognized the centrality of history as a theme in the novel in an influential essay published in 1969,[25] and in the present collection he continues his argument by showing how the *specifically* historical event of the Massacre at Fort William Henry overwhelms Cooper's central characters (and, indeed, his narration) as they virtually disappear from the action during its onslaught. Martin's analysis indicates the degree to which the force of history, sweeping everything before it, makes itself felt in the novel, and the way in which *The Last of the Mohicans*, as a verbal action, replicates that force.

The Massacre at Fort William Henry is also the focus of Robert Lawson-Peebles' essay in this volume. Lawson-Peebles brings a European perspective to bear on this horrific event, showing how its carnage can be understood as a violation of European theories of warfare, and how Cooper, though generally faithful to his historical sources, turned them to his own narrative purposes. As the essays by Martin and Lawson-Peebles make clear in different ways, the Massacre dramatizes vividly the fact that all parties contesting the North American continent in the middle of the eighteenth century – the English and French troops and their Indian allies – were overwhelmed by forces beyond their control.

If the 1980s showed a return to the historical dimensions of *The Last of the Mohicans,* it also exhibited renewed interest in Fiedler's concern with miscegenation in the novel, again with a new twist. For Jane Tompkins, as for Fiedler, the theme of *The Last of the Mohicans* is miscegenation, but of a cultural rather than sexual kind. In viewing the novel as "an agent of cultural formation," she "thinks of *The Last of the Mohicans* as a meditation on *kinds,* and more specifically, as an attempt to calculate exactly how much violation or mixing of its fundamental categories a society can bear."[26]

Shirley Samuels pursues the theme of cultural miscegenation in the present collection, like Tompkins, through a new historicist approach, but she parts decisively with Tompkins' view that the novel ultimately works to restore order by working against that miscegenation. Through close analysis of several key scenes, she demonstrates that *The Last of the Mohicans* "obsessively reiterates such collisions and confusions in its very production of identity, and further, produces identities by a miscegenation of animal and human, natural and cultural." Samuels' approach to *The Last of the Mohicans* also reflects a feminist perspective. She points out that the most disturbing of the novel's confusions of identity is imaged in the Indians' drinking of their female victims' blood during the Massacre; here, according to Samuels, we witness "the extreme form that the fear of women and natural reproduction takes in this novel."

Cooper's novels have not often been analyzed from a feminist perspective, in part because of the historical dominance of "hero-ic" and mythic readings of his work, but Annette Kolodny's 1975 treatment of the Leatherstocking tales identified in them a central feminist issue: how Cooper, through his hero Leatherstocking, can enjoy a forest landscape figured in feminine, pastoral terms without destroying or intruding upon that landscape. In Kolodny's

16

view, *The Last of the Mohicans* represents a precarious and compromised solution to this problem; the novel betrays Cooper's realization "that he could neither accept the guilt of violation [of the feminine landscape] nor free Natty of that guilt."[27]

Feminist criticism of *The Last of the Mohicans* had earlier beginnings, however. Kay Seymour House, in her 1965 study of Cooper, recognized that his female characters, including Cora and Alice Munro, were more complex and interesting than a century of scornful commentary had allowed. A few years later, in 1971, Nina Baym published a key essay extending this line of interpretation. In that essay, Baym analyzed the women characters in the Leatherstocking tales and found them integral to the meanings of the novels. Specifically, Baym recognized that Cooper's women characters "are of central social significance" because marriage is the matrix of his romances, the institution that "takes place within the boundaries of the [social] group" and thus solidifies those boundaries. In this view, the main difference between Alice and Cora Munro is not, as Fiedler had argued, their sexual "lightness" and "darkness"; rather the difference is measured by their implicit social roles. Given Cooper's unswerving commitment to the boundaries of class and group, racially mixed Cora is doomed because "she is both below and above her function," whereas the fainting Alice meets Cooper's (and his culture's) marriageability test with flying colors.[28]

In her essay in this volume, Baym furthers feminist criticism of Cooper by positioning *The Last of the Mohicans* between the works of two women writers of the same period, Lydia Maria Child's *Hobomok* (1824) and Catherine Maria Sedgwick's *Hope Leslie* (1827). Like *The Last of the Mohicans*, these novels explore the relationship between Indians and whites, but their women-centered narratives implicitly challenge Cooper's assumptions about sexual, racial, and social roles.

Some schools of criticism do not fit easily into the developments I have tracked because their concerns with *The Last of the Mohicans* have preoccupied critics steadily from the writer's own time to the present day, and because their emphases have tended to merge with those of other schools. This is true, for example, of pictorial analyses of the novel. The earliest reviewers of *The Last of the Mohicans* were quick to admire its vivid scenic qualities, and even Cooper's detractors in the later nineteenth century and throughout the twentieth century have been willing to acknowledge what D. H. Lawrence called Cooper's "lovely pictures."[29] The excitement stirred in his own time by Cooper's pictures is evidenced by the fact that contemporary landscape and genre painters created numerous scenes from *The Last of the Mohicans;* Thomas Cole, for example, painted at least three such works.

For all the sustained admiration of Cooper's scenic effects in *The Last of the Mohicans* and in his other novels, however, formal and scholarly analysis of these effects did not get fully under way until the 1950s, when James F. Beard published an important essay on the subject. Pointing to the friendships between Cooper and several of his artist contemporaries, including Cole, Beard showed that the novelist had quite consciously employed "the expressive values of painting." This recognition laid the groundwork for other, fuller studies, such as Donald Ringe's book-length treatment of the pictorialism of Bryant, Irving, and Cooper (1971). Ringe's treatment of *The Last of the Mohicans* is essentially thematic, tracking the various meanings of wilderness space that Cooper gives to the novel's rapidly changing and contrasting settings.[30]

Blake Nevius, in his 1976 study of Cooper's landscape aesthetics, sees *The Last of the Mohicans* as a transitional work revealing the novelist's development beyond the abstract topographical artistry of his time to his delineation of "actual scenes." The novel claims its importance, in this view, by virtue of being Cooper's "first imaginative foray into the wilderness [in which] he began to cultivate the art of landscape with a resourcefulness not evident in his earlier romances." *The Last of the Mohicans* is transitional in another sense as well, according to Nevius, because immediately after its publication Cooper went to Europe where he developed "an even more conscious and skillful use of setting" discernible in his later works.[31]

Like pictorial analysis, formalist criticism of *The Last of the Mohicans* is difficult to place historically, but for a different reason: There has been little of it. The New Criticism of the 1930s didn't have much to say about novels generally, and novels of large historical and social import, like Cooper's, were especially unlikely to capture the attention of critics working in this school. Rather, the most important studies of Cooper in the 1930s, such as the work of Spiller and Dorothy Waples, focused on the novels' social and political meanings, revealing the complexity of Cooper's thought and its importance in the development of American life.[32]

One major formalist critic of the 1930s did, however, take up Cooper's work in earnest. This was Yvor Winters, whose 1938 essay took specific issue with Spiller's approach and, in treating the full range of Cooper's novels, significantly raised our estimate of the novelist's "literary virtues." In this brilliant essay, Winters recognized how well crafted and compelling are some of Cooper's lesser known works, such as *The Water Witch*. The limitations of Winters' formalist and didactic criticism, however, when applied to *The Last of the Mohicans*, are apparent in the following passage from his essay: "[T]he style in this work is so consistently florid and redundant that in spite of the action, . . . the book nowhere rises to a level of seriousness. It is curious that the tone of conventional romance which vitiates a great part of [Cooper's] effort should have accumulated so unfortunately here, for there are passages in other books in the series which are not only beautiful but beautiful in a restrained and classical fashion, and which display great richness of moral substance."[33]

In the post–World War II period, a number of critics have undertaken formal analysis of *The Last of the Mohicans*. Donald Darnell's 1965 essay, for example, identifies the novel's *Ubi Sunt* formula by studying its double-journey structure, and Michael D. Butler's 1976 essay examines the relation of historical process to the novel's narrative structure.[34] As both these essays illustrate, however, most contemporary criticism of this kind puts formal analysis at the service of larger mythic or historical interpretations. And it remains true that Cooper's work has never undergone the intense formal analysis that has been applied to the fiction of other nineteenth-century American writers such as Nathaniel Hawthorne and Herman Melville. The lessons of formalist criticism, however, have not been lost in Cooper studies in our time. The best practitioners of all contemporary approaches to *The Last of the Mohicans* exhibit close and responsible attention to the text. For example,

the focused examination of language characteristic of new historicist approaches bears little resemblance to the broad thematic
generalizations of Parrington's traditional historicism.

Whatever varying emphases different schools of criticism have
given to *The Last of the Mohicans* since the end of World War II, one
thing is clear. No longer is it possible to regard this book simply as
a well made adventure story. Because the novel, historically, has
made so large a claim on our imaginations as a breathlessly exciting narrative, it has had to wait longer than others of Cooper's
major works for critics to begin discerning in it deeper meanings
and implications. This is the central irony in the history of the
book's reception by readers. As the essays in the present collection
illustrate, however, critics in our time understand that *The Last of
the Mohicans,* as much as any novel Cooper wrote, reveals the full
complexity of his imagination and expresses his deepest hopes and
fears for the American experiment.

NOTES

1. See the commentary by Cooper's daughter Susan Fenimore Cooper,
   in *The Cooper Gallery; or, Pages and Pictures from the Writings of James
   Fenimore Cooper, with Notes* (New York: James Miller, 1865), p. 146.
   See also James Beard, "Afterword" to *The Last of the Mohicans* (New
   York: New American Library, 1962), p. 420.
2. Susan Fenimore Cooper, pp. 322–3.
3. Despite Cooper's claims for accuracy of representation in this first
   preface, however, he considerably altered the facts of Indian allegiances and tribal identities for thematic purposes. For an excellent
   brief study of these alterations, see John McWilliams, "The Historical
   Context of *The Last of the Mohicans,*" in *The Last of the Mohicans,* ed.
   McWilliams (New York: Oxford University Press, 1990), pp. 355–63;
   see also Ian K. Steele, "Cooper and Clio: The Sources for 'A Narrative
   of 1757,'" *Canadian Review of American Studies* 20 (Winter 1989):
   121–35.
4. A useful gathering of contemporary reviews of *The Last of the
   Mohicans,* and others of Cooper's novels, is *Fenimore Cooper: The Critical Heritage,* ed. George Dekker and John P. McWilliams (London:
   Routledge and Kegan Paul, 1973). For the convenience of readers,
   quotations from such reviews are, wherever possible, cited from this

volume, in which full citations for their original publication sources can be found. For the passages quoted here, see pp. 83, 112, 113.

5. Lewis Cass, "Structure of the Indian Languages," *North American Review* 26 (April 1828): 376; Bird, *Nick of the Woods*, ed. Curtis Dahl (New Haven: College and University Press, 1967; orig. pub.1835); see Bird's "Preface to the Revised Edition" (1853), pp. 31–5; Parkman, "The Works of James Fenimore Cooper," *North American Review* 74 (January 1852): 150.
6. Dekker and McWilliams, p. 282.
7. W. C. Brownell, *American Prose Masters: Cooper, Hawthorne, Emerson, Poe, Lowell, Henry James*, ed. Howard Mumford Jones (Cambridge, Mass.: Harvard University Press, 1967; orig. pub. 1909), pp. 16, 19; Georg Friden, *James Fenimore Cooper and Ossian*, Essays and Studies on American Language and Literature, American Institute of the University of Uppsala, 8 (Uppsala and Cambridge, Mass., 1949).
8. Brownell, p. 17.
9. Richard Slotkin, "Introduction" to *The Last of the Mohicans* (New York: Penguin, 1987), p. xxv.
10. For example, see Philip Fisher's discussion of Cooper in *Hard Facts: Setting and Form in the American Novel* (Oxford: Oxford University Press, 1987), esp. his analysis of *The Deerslayer* in chap. 1. For an interesting recent reconsideration of *The Pioneers*, raising related issues from a new historicist perspective, see Thomas Hill Schaub, " 'Cut in Plain Marble': The Language of the Tomb in *The Pioneers*," in *The Green American Tradition: Essays and Poems for Sherman Paul*, ed. H. Daniel Peck (Baton Rouge: Louisiana State University Press, 1989), pp. 58–74.
11. James Beard, "Historical Introduction" to the State University of New York Press edition of *The Last of the Mohicans*, p. xviii. It should be pointed out, however, that in his book of social analysis, *Notions of the Americans*, published in 1828, Cooper did give qualified support to the policy of Indian removal.
12. See, for example, my *A World by Itself: The Pastoral Moment in Cooper's Fiction* (New Haven: Yale University Press, 1977), esp. p. 141.
13. Sayre, *Thoreau and the American Indians* (Princeton: Princeton University Press, 1977).
14. Dekker and McWilliams, pp. 90, 10.
15. Thomas R. Lounsbury, *James Fenimore Cooper* (Boston: Houghton Mifflin, 1883), p. 53; James Grossman, *James Fenimore Cooper* (Stanford: Stanford University Press, 1967), p. 44. This judgment of *The Last of the Mohicans* was shared by a number of notable critics in

the first half of the twentieth century, including Alexander Cowie,
Yvor Winters, and Van Wyck Brooks.

16. D. H. Lawrence, *Studies in Classic American Literature* (New York: Viking, 1961; orig. pub. by Thomas Seltzer, 1923), pp. 48–54, 59.

17. R. W. B. Lewis, *The American Adam: Innocence and Tragedy in the Nineteenth Century* (Chicago: University of Chicago Press, 1955), pp. 98–105; Henry Nash Smith, *Virgin Land: The American West as Symbol and Myth* (Cambridge, Mass.: Harvard University Press, 1950), chap. 6; Joel Porte, *The Romance in America: Studies in Cooper, Poe, Hawthorne, Melville, and James* (Middletown, Conn.: Wesleyan University Press, 1969), esp. pp. 18–22, 39–41; Roy Harvey Pearce, "The Leatherstocking Tales Re-examined," *South Atlantic Quarterly* 46 (1947): 524–36; Edwin Fussell, *Frontier: American Literature and the American West* (Princeton: Princeton University Press, 1965), pp. 27–68.

18. Leslie Fiedler, *Love and Death in the American Novel*, rev. ed. (New York: Dell, 1966), pp. 208, 205, 207; first published in New York by Criterion in 1960.

19. George Dekker, *James Fenimore Cooper: the Novelist* (London: Routledge and Kegan Paul, 1967), p. 68; Donald Davie, *The Heyday of Sir Walter Scott* (London: Routledge and Kegan Paul, 1961).

20. Thomas Philbrick, "*The Last of the Mohicans* and the Sounds of Discord," *American Literature* 36 (March 1971): 40, 25.

21. Ibid., 25.

22. Peck, *A World by Itself*, pp. 89–145; Stephen Railton, *Fenimore Cooper: A Study of His Life and Imagination* (Princeton: Princeton University Press, 1978), pp. 34–6; Wayne Franklin, *The New World of James Fenimore Cooper* (Chicago: University of Chicago Press, 1982), p. 245.

23. An exception is a structuralist/linguistic analysis of the novel by Dennis W. Allen, "'By All the Truth of Signs': James Fenimore Cooper's *The Last of the Mohicans*," *Studies in American Fiction* 9 (Autumn 1981): 159–79.

24. Vernon L. Parrington, *Main Currents in American Thought, Volume Two: The Romantic Revolution, 1800–1860* (New York: Harcourt, Brace, 1927), pp. 214–29; Robert E. Spiller, *Fenimore Cooper: Critic of His Times* (New York: Minton, Balch, 1931); William P. Kelly, *Plotting America's Past: Fenimore Cooper and the Leatherstocking Tales* (Carbondale: Southern Illinois University Press, 1983), pp. 45–84.

25. Terence Martin, "From the Ruins of History: *The Last of the Mohicans*," *Novel: A Forum on Fiction* 2 (Spring 1969): 221–9.

26. Jane Tompkins, *Sensational Designs: The Cultural Work of American Fic-

tion, 1790–1860 (New York: Oxford University Press, 1985), pp. 119, 106.

27. Annette Kolodny, *The Lay of the Land: Metaphor as Experience and History in American Life and Letters* (Chapel Hill: University of North Carolina Press, 1975), p. 101.

28. Kay Seymour House, *Cooper's Americans* (Columbus: Ohio State University Press, 1965), chap. 1; Nina Baym, "The Women of Cooper's Leatherstocking Tales," *American Quarterly* 23 (December 1971): 697, 698, 705. One of the nineteenth century's most influential attacks on Cooper's women characters was that of James Russell Lowell, who, in his *A Fable for Critics,* wrote: "And the women he draws from one model don't vary, / All sappy as maples and flat as a prairie" (Dekker and McWilliams, p. 239).

29. Lawrence, p. 55.

30. James Beard, "Cooper and His Artistic Contemporaries," *New York History* 35 (1954): 491; Donald Ringe, *The Pictorial Mode: Space and Time in the Art of Bryant, Irving, and Cooper* (Lexington: University Press of Kentucky), pp. 43–7.

31. Blake Nevius, *Cooper's Landscapes: An Essay on the Picturesque Vision* (Berkeley: University of California Press, 1976), pp. 13–14.

32. Spiller, op. cit.; Dorothy Waples, *The Whig Myth of James Fenimore Cooper* (New Haven: Yale University Press, 1938). For an important reexamination of Cooper's work for its political and social meanings, see John P. McWilliams, Jr., *Political Justice in a Republic: James Fenimore Cooper's America* (Berkeley: University of California Press, 1972).

33. Yvor Winters, "Fenimore Cooper, or the Ruins of Time," in *Maule's Curse* (Norfolk, Conn.: New Directions, 1938), pp. 25, 36.

34. Donald Darnell, "Uncas as Hero: The *Ubi Sunt* Formula in *The Last of the Mohicans,*" *American Literature* 37 (November 1965): 259–66; Michael D. Butler, "Narrative Structure and Historical Process in *The Last of the Mohicans,*" *American Literature* 48 (1976): 117–39.

2

The Wilderness of Words in
The Last of the Mohicans

WAYNE FRANKLIN

WHERE did James Fenimore Cooper find the wilderness into which he sent his characters with the very first sentence of *The Last of the Mohicans?* It is a wilderness, we quickly learn, whose "toils and dangers" pose almost as grave a threat for those characters as do the bloody enemies who await them there, a world where "impervious . . . forests" painfully delay – though they cannot eliminate, such is the devotion to violence in this book – the fearful meeting of the opposing hosts (p. 11). And it is a wilderness, to begin to answer my question, whose like Cooper could not have found in any book he had written heretofore.

There were some hints in his five earlier novels. As I have argued elsewhere, *The Pioneers* (1823) holds a powerfully originating place among all Cooper's works because it introduces not only Natty Bumppo but also the crucial theme of border settlement.[1] This combination almost inevitably would push Cooper's imagination beyond the "clearing": The 1826 novel, showing the same hero before the coming of settlement, was latent in the 1823 one. Furthermore, both *The Pioneers* and *The Spy* (1821) – whose wandering patriot Harvey Birch in some ways anticipates the indefatigable Hawkeye – flirt more directly with the wilderness, hinting at Cooper's uneasy sense that his future as a writer did not lie with the domestic themes that apparently dominate his early novels. It was not the Moseleys of *Precaution* (1820), the Whartons of *The Spy,* or even the Temple establishment of *The Pioneers* around which his art was to shape itself, but rather the fugitive characters who occupied the spatial and social edges of these tales. If he could not often attack his genteel characters to their faces, he seldom avoided a chance to knife them from the rear with the stiff blade of their own gentility. Rarely do the underclass characters in his books prove as blind as their nominal betters.

Yet if *The Spy* and *The Pioneers* do not insulate their genteel characters completely from the roughness that environs their fragile social order, neither do they embrace that roughness wholeheartedly. The edges remain distant from the centers, marginal domains even if important ones. *The Spy,* though it makes important use of the physical world where Harvey Birch proves both his self-regarding skills and his selfless devotion to America, thus exploits a quite European definition of the frontier. Its "neutral ground" divides not the settlements from the woods – as did the classic American frontier – but rather England from America, the past of colonial dependence from the independent national future. If we approach the idea of the "wild" at all in this book, we do so not by departing from one space and entering another but rather by leaving behind the ideals of Birch or "Harper" to explore the withering realities of the Skinners.[2]

To be sure, *The Spy* does present us with the very first of Cooper's many "Indians," but they exist only in the overheated mind of a British clergyman who fears he may be scalped as he trips about in his frock in the Westchester countryside. "The Indians – they who do nothing but rob, murder, and destroy," surely must be lurking nearby, he tells Captain Lawton, who responds by instructing the Briton in American geography, both physical and moral. There are no actual Indians nearby, for the wilderness is far away. On the other hand, the "woods and rocks" around them indeed do harbor "enemies," namely, the Skinners, "whose mouths are filled with liberty and equality, and whose hearts are overflowing with cupidity and gall." Probably because he has confused "skinners" and "scalpers," the Briton admits that he had thought the American guerrillas were themselves Indians. When Lawton answers, "You did the savages injustice," Cooper is underscoring his sense of the moral ambiguity of the Revolution, this most American of wars. But he also is distancing the "Neutral Ground" from the literal frontier he was to explore in *The Last of the Mohicans.*[3] Violence here is not spatially conditioned, important as space is to the novel.

Even in *The Pioneers,* in which the woods and the violence possible there impinge on the clearing, Cooper tended to return his action to the safe middle ground of Templeton instead of pushing it irretrievably toward the wild land. In its last, most "active" stages, this "Descriptive Tale" is centered by a series of backward glances that tie the forest scenes visually and spatially to the awkward but at the same time reassuring terrain of the village. The settlers know where they are because the way back to Templeton is always known and open to them, regardless of the wild threats that may challenge them in the woods. They are not terminally disoriented: Their cognitive maps, so to speak, remain intact, securing their positions and identities though danger may environ them.[4] As with Cooper's other settlement tales, from *The Wept of Wish-ton-Wish* (1829) to *The Crater* (1847), the clarity of his narrative in *The Pioneers* depends on the commitment of his own eye to the clearing. There is even something mildly phobic about the manner in which these stories ignore the wild space around their centers, clinging to the civil ground despite the fact that the very meaning of that civil ground derives from its contrast with the wilds. Although shipwrecked in the midst of the lonely Pacific, his two main characters in *The Crater* thus are able not only to find their way home but also to return to their island and there reconstruct America in almost every detail – from snoopy newspapermen to obnoxious demagogues – to reconstruct it so thoroughly, in fact, that their alter-America ruins Paradise, the transported "center" destroying the remote "edge." The natural disaster that ends *The Crater* is the consequence of social and political ills, not the assault of nature against a just human order tentatively planted in it. As with *The Spy,* the wildness dwells in the heart of society.[5]

In *The Last of the Mohicans* we encounter space without such centers, just or not. It is space rawly imagined, fearfully projected, as if Cooper saw in the chaos of his subject some exciting and at the same time frightening reflection of his own imaginative energies.[6] If Cooper did not find this wilderness already emergent in the way space is constructed in his earlier fiction, where then did he find it?

He began to find it, in the most literal sense, in the lingering wilderness of New York. In Otsego County there was plenty of rough country during his boyhood. But when his sister Hannah

27

wrote that James and his brothers "are very wild and show plainly they have been bred in the Woods,"[7] she was pleasantly overstating the case: already by the census of 1800, a mere fifteen years after settlement began in earnest in Otsego and the year in which James was to turn eleven, it was the largest of New York's "western" counties and the tenth largest among all the state's counties, new or old. Ten years later, only two counties in the state – Dutchess and New York, both long established in the lower Hudson valley – had more population than Otsego.[8] If there were ample "woods" in Cooper's home county, as Hannah averred, it was the clearing that dominated the landscape.

Indeed, so little did Cooper himself see of the initial period of settlement in Otsego that later in life he claimed it was not there but at Oswego, on Lake Ontario, that he had gained "most of [his] notions of a new country."[9] Statistics of the time tend to support Cooper's perception that Oswego lay closer to the ambiguous American border than Otsego in the same period.[10] It remains true, however, that not even Oswego in 1808–1809, when Cooper was with the navy there, was really frontier territory, let alone a wilderness pure and simple. Like the "Neutral Ground" of *The Spy,* Oswego at the time resembled a European frontier more than an American one. Indeed, Oswego had long been a site of contention among competing European and native groups, as Cooper's own experience certainly brought to his attention. Oswego was the locus of considerable political tension. Not only was the "rumour of War" with England "strong" there (as Cooper wrote home in 1808)[11] – for England's Canadian possessions lay just across the lake – but the Americans living there were battling their own central government as well. The Embargo Act of 1807, prohibiting all foreign commerce, was a dead letter in Oswego, which traded heavily with Canada; Cooper's own naval duties were involved with the effort to put an end to such illicit traffic. He was fighting with his own countrymen even as he anticipated fighting for them against the British. When he described the population of Oswego to his brother Richard in November of 1808, he said the place "has been crowded with company for this last month – officers – merchants – smugglers &c &c – ."[12] It was more like a military post crossed with an entrepot and a smuggler's den than a wilderness backwater. The hottest issue there in 1808 and 1809 was foreign relations, not clearing the forest.

Perhaps some taste of what the "Neutral Ground" of West-chester had been like during the 1770s and 1780s came to Cooper here at this other ambiguous space between jurisdictions, where greed overcame patriotism and one could never be quite sure where peoples' allegiances lay. It is instructive that he chose to end *The Spy* not in revolutionary Westchester but rather on the Niagara frontier of the War of 1812. This was ground he had seen in 1808 and 1809, ground – and water – he was to return to more cen-trally, of course, in *The Pathfinder* (1840). That he found Oswego "one of the pleasantest situations in the world" in 1808 suggests that, whatever its ambiguities then, the village and its fort were not so deeply buried in the woods as Mabel Dunham's solitary block-house was to be in that later novel.[13] The "wilderness" of *The Last of the Mohicans* was not transcribed by Cooper from his memories of the Oswego region: The "Horican" was not a relocated Ontario.

Similar hesitations might be registered even regarding Cooper's use of the "Horican" itself. He first visited Lake George and other parts of his setting in the upper Hudson valley in 1824 with four touring Britons, and it was during this tour – indeed, just as Cooper and one of the Englishmen stood "in the caverns at Glens falls" – that Cooper had "determined to write the book."[14] This anecdote, expanded on by Cooper's daughter Susan, is well known, but how the visit of 1824 affected his development of the book's wild setting deserves more consideration than it usually receives. Cooper tried to claim that these northern regions retained even in his own day much of their wilderness character. In his 1831 "In-troduction" to the Bentley edition of the novel, he wrote that since the time of the book's action the locale had "undergone as little change . . . as almost any other district of equal extent within the whole limits of the United States." There were, he conceded, "fashionable and well-attended watering-places" around the spring where Natty paused to drink, as well as roads where in Natty's time not even paths had cut through the forest. "Glenn's has a large village," he went on, and although both William Henry and a later fort lay in ruins at the lake, a village stood there now. "But beyond this," he concluded in 1831, "the enterprise and energy of a people who have done so much in other places have done little here. The whole of that wilderness, in which the latter incidents of the legend occurred is nearly a wilderness still" (pp. 7–8).

That "nearly" was an important qualifier, as contemporary evidence makes clear. In some ways the Adirondack region to which Cooper referred in his final sentence *had* been passed over as settlers sought out better land farther west, in the "new countries" of Cooper's home state or in the vast regions beyond. Especially in the upper Hudson valley and near Lake George and Lake Champlain, however, the landscape had hardly escaped the furious process of change visited upon so many nominally wild areas of the nation from the 1780s to the 1830s. The ultimate source of the Hudson on Mt. Marcy was not located until after the first transcontinental railroad had been completed in 1869, yet at Glens Falls, even when Cooper himself visited the cavern, evidence of substantial change literally covered the landscape.

Poet and Yale president Timothy Dwight, who visited the village several times, found a dam across both channels already in 1798, standing eight or ten feet high and abutting the island in the middle of the falls. This dam supplied power for "a long train of mills on the north and a small number on the south bank," the two shores connected by a bridge anchored at its center on the island.[15] When he saw the falls in later years he found the soft rock much altered by weathering (a point Cooper also remarked), and the immediate vicinity of the impressive cataract, as well as the landscape all the way from Albany north, considerably changed by human use. At times he descanted on the increasing transformation of the terrain, as in these comments from 1811:

> The country from Albany to Lake George is extensively improved. Waterford is become a handsome village of about one hundred and fifty houses, surrounding a neat Presbyterian church, many of them valuable. . . . On the road from Waterford to Fort Edward a great number of valuable houses are erected. The enclosures are improved and multiplied, and the country is more generally and better cultivated. . . . [T]hroughout the whole distance, the country is greatly advanced toward a state of thorough cultivation. At Fort Edward, Sandy Hill, and Glens Falls, there are three handsome

villages, greatly improved in every respect since my last journey through this region.[16]

As to Lake George, when Dwight visited it in 1802 he observed that "to complete the scenery belonging to this fine piece of water the efforts of cultivation were wanting." Always enamored of the middle landscape where rural life gave an orderly finish to nature, Dwight clearly liked Lake George in the wild but would like it even better once it was tamed. Understandably, he was delighted a mere nine years later with the vicinity's sudden "improvements." He had thought a half century would be required before "the villas of opulence and refinement" would "add . . . the elegances of art to the beauty and majesty of nature." In 1811 there had already been "raised up a beautiful village, exhibiting, with a brilliancy almost singular, many of these elegancies," a village with a "more cheerful and thrifty appearance" than most settlements its size.[17] As with the larger landscape from Albany north as he had seen it on earlier visits, Dwight here found strong evidence that the nation was establishing its physical possession of nature.

For the most part, Dwight applauded the signs of change he read throughout the region. In 1811, however, he found the cataract at Glens Falls woefully defaced by human use, as much as or even more than by natural change:

> To my great mortification I found it encumbered and defaced by the erection of several paltry buildings, raised up since my last visit to this place. The rocks, both above and below the bridge, were extremely altered, and greatly for the worse, by the operations of the water and the weather. The courses of the currents had undergone in many places a similar variation. The view at the same time was broken by the buildings, two or three of which, designed to be mills, were given up as useless and were in ruins. Another was a wretched-looking cottage, standing upon the island between the bridges. Nothing could be more dissonant from the splendor of this scene, and hardly anything more disgusting. I found a considerable part of the rocks below the road so much wasted that I could scarcely acknowledge them to be the same.[18]

This scene hardly offers a hopeful view of America's emerging maturity. But for an understanding of Cooper it is the abundance of human signs in Dwight's landscapes, not their particular virtue in his eye, that is important. Clearly, the landscape Cooper visited in 1824 and chose as the setting for his first "wilderness" novel was not in any real sense a wilderness any longer. Recovering the old wilderness was not necessarily an easy task. The cataract was becoming so obscured with human structures in these years that historian Francis Parkman, when he visited it in 1842, was more disquieted by what he saw there than by the sloppy landscapes of Albany and Schenectady, which his New England eye had found quite "disgusting":

> [M]y wrath mounted higher yet at the sight of that noble cataract almost concealed under a huge, awkward bridge, thrown directly across it, with the addition of a dam above, and about twenty mills of various kinds. Add to all, that the current was choked by masses of [lumbermen's] drift logs above and below, and that a dirty village lined the banks of the river on both sides, and some idea may possibly be formed of the way in which the New Yorkers have bedevilled Glens.[19]

Cooper himself, crowding the island with his implacable Mingoes, was to *be-devil* "Glenn's" in a quite different sense. Before he could do that, however, he had to exorcise the other demons that possessed the place. Whether written over with a fine hand or merely scrawled upon, this region bore indelible proof of human occupation, proof which cannot have escaped Cooper's attention in 1824. He and the Britons with whom he traveled must have crossed the rickety bridge mentioned by Dwight (Parkman's more offensive one was erected later) in order to get out to the island and the caverns that honeycombed it. They must have found mills and other buildings cluttering the banks and perhaps even the island, not to mention the dam that cut across the stream like a straightedge, raising the water level somewhat and thus increasing the height of the drop in the Hudson, but jarring with the wonderful jumble of the cataract's natural lines. Cooper had never seen the place in its wilder condition, and therefore could draw neither on the falls as he saw them nor on earlier memories. The accumulating example of his previous books – his private rhetoric, one might say – offered little help. He did not know the wilderness and yet plunged headlong into it as he wrote *The Last of the*

Mohicans. Where, one must ask, did he find the wilderness as he worked on that novel in 1825?

The answer is complex. He found it not by rendering a concrete historical landscape or copying and elaborating on some scene from an earlier book, but rather by erasing history from nature. The act of doing so was a crucial one in his art, an act he was to perform again and again over the years. Ultimately, I want to consider what that act meant, but first I want to investigate how it was performed.

In the case of the Glens Falls scene, it is as if he held the falls in his mind's eye and, object by object, removed the accumulated burden of culture from the place until he got down to the rock that underpinned it all. He found the wilderness, in other words, *under* the nation. How well he succeeded is suggested by an incidental use of the falls during the course of the siege there. Natty and his party, we recall, have holed up in the cavern that penetrates the island downstream from the cataract. In their efforts to capture Natty and the others, the Mingoes try various expedients. Among other things, a number of them push out into the river above the falls and, directing themselves toward the island, seek to land at its upper point:

> Heyward lifted his head from the cover, and beheld what he justly considered a prodigy of rashness and skill. The river had worn away the edge of the soft rock in such a manner, as to render its first pitch less abrupt and perpendicular, than is usual at waterfalls. With no other guide than the ripple of the stream where it met the head of the island, a party of their insatiable foes had ventured into the current, and swam down upon this point, knowing the ready access it would give, if successful, to their intended victims. As Hawk-eye ceased speaking, four human heads could be seen peering above a few logs of drift wood, that had lodged on these naked rocks, and which had probably suggested the idea of the practicability of the hazardous undertaking. At the next moment, a fifth form was seen floating over the green edge of the fall, a little from the line of the island. The savage struggled powerfully to gain the point of safety, and favoured by the glancing water, he was already stretching forth an arm to meet the grasp of his companions, when he shot away again with the whirling current, appeared to rise into the air, with uplifted arms, and startling eye-balls, and fell, with a sudden

plunge, into that deep and yawning abyss over which he hovered. A single, wild, despairing shriek, rose from the cavern, and all was hushed again as the grave. (p. 69)

This is a masterfully imagined scene. Note how well Cooper has thought his way into the landscape. There is, to begin with, an effective shifting back and forth across the space that separates the Munro party from its pursuers. Although Cooper first presents the episode from Heyward's perspective, he soon attempts to imagine how an Indian eye must apprehend it: Hence his nice touch about the "ripple" that guides the five warriors. Quickly we are back inside Heyward's viewpoint once more, seeing the "four human heads" that peer over the logs at the major, only to shift back just as quickly to the natives again — sensing how the logs over which they now are peering must have suggested to them, as they clung to the shore above, the whole hazardous project. This shifting of perspectives gives the landscape here a strong three-dimensionality. It is as if Cooper triangulates his own omniscient stance by using first one and then the other limited point of view. As a result, we become acutely aware of space in this scene. It is, first, a practical fact of experience, something to be carefully dealt with, as the Indians must deal with it here. And it is a kind of mystery, a profoundly limiting condition of perception, indeed, of life itself.

Adding special force to Cooper's articulation of these themes is the real grace with which he invents the death of the fifth member of the party. The "green edge" of the fall, the single arm hopefully stretched out for help, the thrust of his body into the air as the man goes over, the useless uplift now of both his arms, the flash of his eyes, the despair of his shriek, the silence of his end — although the viewpoint is Heyward's rather than the Indian's, these seem to measure the cataract from the inside, as it were, not as a feature of some painterly landscape but as a bodily fact with definite consequences for humanity. Timothy Dwight confided in one of his manuscript notebooks that Glens Falls left him almost speechless: "I never met with an object which I thought it more difficult to describe than this cataract. The pencil ought to be employed in exhibiting this piece of scenery and even that would find no small difficulty in forming a likeness."[20] Cooper succeeds where Dwight (the man who, incidentally, had expelled him from Yale in 1805) failed. Cooper succeeds by portraying the falls not as an "object" but rather as an experienced terrain, not via the eye but the body. His rendering here is kinesthetic.

Cooper's achievement is all the more impressive because he saw the falls only once; Dwight returned many times to the scene, struggling to get the view down on paper in version after version. Furthermore, whereas Dwight was attempting merely to describe what he saw, Cooper had to invent what no one could see anymore — the falls as a natural fact unburdened by human signs. The falls as Cooper saw them in 1824 must have been so altered that his dramatic mapping of the spot in the novel depended on radical erasures. Very little came to him from direct observation. The island in the middle of the stream, for instance, must no longer have had much of a "point," for the location of the dam would have cut across the island's head as it connected the two shores. Hence Cooper imagined that point into being, so to speak, and imagined the ripple of the river marking it. Though the drift logs conceivably came to him from the clutter the lumber milling at Glens Falls spewed into the river, one notes how different are his drift logs in the novel from the ones Parkman was to find so offensive. Cooper uses them as a prop helping him move back to some earlier condition of this landscape and invents a fitting action for it, not as a symbol of how unattainable the pristine past is. From this one probable hint he found in the 1824 landscape, Cooper had to bring the river back to its original state on his own, in his mind, before using it as the setting for his beautiful, if horrifying, episode. He had to erase the signs of human possession from nature in order to find the clean slate of his wilderness.

Throughout the novel he erased such signs wherever he found them, reducing the European presence on the face of America at every turn. In some instances, his nominal erasures restored some older human order. For example, he reimagined Fort William Henry in Chapter 14:

> Directly on the shore of the lake, and nearer to its western than to its eastern margin, lay the extensive earthen ramparts and low build-

ings of William Henry. Two of the sweeping bastions appeared to rest on the water, which washed their bases, while a deep ditch and extensive morasses guarded its other sides and angles. The land had been cleared of wood for a reasonable distance around the work, but every other part of the scene lay in the green livery of nature, except where the limpid water mellowed the view, or the bold rocks thrust their black and naked heads above the undulating outlines of the mountain ranges. (p. 141)

Given the ruins that Cooper saw when he visited Lake George in 1824, this is as impressive a reimagining as any in the novel. He often reconstructed past scenes masterfully in his historical romances, as with his magnificent recreation of revolutionary Boston and the battle of Bunker Hill just one year earlier in *Lionel Lincoln* (1825). Yet the reimagining here is a frail thing. Soon a fog rolls up the lake as the sun rises, obliterating the French camp from view and then enveloping the fort with almost magical speed. Suddenly the wanderers lose the mountaintop panorama that has made the landscape lie passive as "a map beneath their feet" (p. 141). So disoriented are Natty and the Mohicans, accomplished guides though they may be, that they cannot tell where the massive fort is, and so almost rush, by mistake, into the enemy encampment. Cooper seems to have rebuilt the fort only to snatch the hasty image rather cruelly from the eyes of his characters, abandoning them as he does that Huron who fruitlessly tries to grasp the hands thrust out toward him. Natty's attempt to follow the trail of cannonballs toward the fort, ludicrous as it seems at first, may just be Cooper's way of emphasizing how confused the wanderers are, how collapsed is the cognitive design of this world. There is, here in the wilds, no glimpse back at some central ordering village, no road the eye can travel, no secure hand to save the lost. Where such spatial clearings are gone the mind itself seems lacking in clarity.

Besides, as every reader knows, the fort that Cooper found in ruins in 1824 has been reimagined in the novel so that it may be ruined again. Cooper rebuilds it only to burn it, recovering its text, so to speak, only to erase it again in the course of his narrative. And what an erasure the book's climax is! It is not merely the physical structure of William Henry that is reduced, but even more gruesomely its human inhabitants. In the most grisly scene in all Cooper's works, the British leave the fort as a "confused and timid throng" worthy of Dante: "The whole . . . was in motion; the weak and wounded, groaning, and in suffering; their comrades, silent, and sullen; and the women and children in terror, they knew not of what" (p. 174). The erasure begins with a single child whose head – as in the stylized annihilations of the captivity narrative – is "dashed . . . against a rock," reduced from a babe-in-arms to nothing, "quivering remains," an "unseemly object." As among the wicked of the Bible, so among the wicked of this book mercy is a kind of cruelty: soon the same Indian turned on the mother and "mercifully drove his tomahawk into her own brain," felling her to grasp after the babe in death as she had in life (p. 175).

These are the only two deaths that Cooper renders directly in the chapter. "Death was every where" (p. 176), he writes, but being everywhere death is no one place. Instead of a language of violence we thus have a language of horror, of effect rather than act. With what at first may seem a kind of mercy of his own, Cooper recovers few details of the massacre, satisfied with the bloody light his prose casts on events it does not name. Despite the bloodiness of the prose, his is a language of inner anxiety rather than outward fear; there are few correlatives for its emotions. In some ways, the omission of acts even as he retains their effects heightens the pitch of the scene. Adding to its overwrought tone, the horror is oddly spiced with irony: Cooper compares the yells that echo Magua's "fatal and appalling whoop" to the presumably more celestial (if no more comforting) "blasts of the final summons" (p. 176); Magua, holding up his "reeking hand," comments on both its color and his own violence, saying, with a wit that seems out of place here, "It is red, but it comes from white veins!" (p. 178). Gamut insists that his "death song" (p. 177) will protect the Munro women, whereas its first effect is to allow Magua, hearing it, to find them in the tumult and take them prisoner. Magua shows himself to be a strangely dainty brute, passing up the ordinary whites whom he might massacre to find "some victim more worthy of his renown" (p. 177); Gamut seems to Magua "a subject too worthless even to destroy" (p. 178): The singer will survive only because no one takes the trouble to kill him. Cora and Alice

37

are terrified by the violence about them but not appalled by it, and so look back down on the Massacre from the mountain partly from fascination, from "the curiosity which seems inseparable from horror" (p. 179).[21] The violence subsides not when all the potential victims are dead, but rather when loot becomes more appealing than bloodshed ("cupidity," Cooper acerbically writes, "got the mastery of revenge" [p. 179]). Finally, we learn that the victims' "cries of horror" do not simply subside into silence, but are "drowned" in the triumphant "whoops" of the savages (p. 179), the blend of pain and exultation giving a quite eerie end to the flood of noise with which Cooper assaults the reader's ears throughout the chapter. Cooper creates horror here, but he is not only horrified by the action of the scene; he is, like the Munros, fascinated, intrigued, "curious" as well. If we do not have much in the way of a blow-by-blow rendering of the violence, neither do we have an author piously cushioning the victims or his audience from the rough wit of history. There is a kind of ghoulishness in the chapter, and in the book as a whole – a holdover, in some ways, from the midnight Gothicism of *Lionel Lincoln*.

All of this suggests that Cooper turned his hand – and with some relish, not just as an exercise in negative capability – to what he calls with terse but considerable irony the "cruel work" (p. 179) of the Massacre. He claims in the chapter following that he had "rather incidentally mentioned than described" the "bloody and inhuman scene" at William Henry (p. 180). But that claim is an evasion. It implies that the episode simply *had* to be touched on; the author might have wished to pass it over, but after all it was "conspicuous in the pages of colonial history" (p. 180) and hence could not be erased from this historically inclined "Narrative of 1757." A moment's reflection will remind us that insofar as the episode forms part of the action of the novel, it is there because – history notwithstanding – Cooper the novelist chose to put it there, just as he chose to set his novel during the French and Indian War. More important, the claim is false to the book. If the Massacre is not described in great detail, his treatment of it is in some ways more devastating, certainly more horrifying, than a stenographic report would be. So, too, the dominant bloody mood of the whole book, unrivaled elsewhere in his work, suggests an aesthetic not of restraint but of perverse indulgence.[22] Cooper must have known that he was working on the sensibility of his reader with a masterful blend of sudden death, veiled hints of sexual violence, and a lingering apprehensiveness that sets his prose on edge for much of the book. It is a book scratched with a fingernail on the blackboard of his reader's consciousness.

To make my claim another way, Cooper must have known that he had to find his wilderness setting not in the literal American landscape but rather within the human psyche. What he really erased to find it was the whole construction of polite society with which Euro-Americans (as Dwight, say, may be taken to testify here) were inscribing the face of America. To erase that construction Cooper removed the signs of order from the physical space of his tale. More important, he removed the restraints of "mannerly" fiction from his book.

He did so by creating a singularly mixed work. Terence Martin's observation about the brief pause in the book's action just before the Massacre seems to me to apply much more generally to the novel. The sudden absence of Natty and the Mohicans from the action in these chapters, Martin writes, marks "a radical change" in the sort of book Cooper is creating – we have here "an interlude of domestic fiction."[23] In fact, the book is structured throughout – almost sentence-by-sentence – by a switching back and forth between the codes suitable for "domestic fiction" and those that emerge from the forest, between, in Thomas Philbrick's terms, the pious and beautiful psalms of David and the horrid yells of the Mingoes.[24] The wilderness is heard as much as seen, this being part of Cooper's masterful Gothicism, his displacement of the reader's fear with anxiety; the text of polite speech and genteel attitude is erased by, or perhaps "drowned in," the yells, shrieks, cries, groans, and war whoops that echo through the forest. Speech is replaced by mere noise; the wilderness comes into being within the language of the book, precisely at those moments when the logic of the domestic novel is brutally countered by the violence of Cooper's forest. Moreover, the effects of this process are felt on an extremely local level. The wilderness emerges, for instance, in a passage such as: "The manhood of Heyward felt no shame, in dropping tears over this spectacle of affectionate rapture; and

Uncas stood, fresh and blood-stained from the combat, a calm, and apparently, an unmoved looker-on" (p. 115). If one function of the rest of this sentence is to show the gradual ennobling of Uncas by his awakening love for Cora – and hence the "civilizing" of this one "savage" – below that conscious ideology Cooper himself moves in the opposite direction. To describe Uncas as both *fresh* and at the same time *blood-stained* is to break the control that Heyward's decorum, nominally dominating the scene, only seems to exert here. It is to insert the wilderness into white prose.

Nor does Cooper merely insert the wilderness into tame speech. He breaks the latter off any number of times in the book, silencing it with noise:

> "And did he [Col. Munro] not speak of me, Heyward?" demanded Alice, with jealous affection. "Surely, he forgot not altogether his little Elsie!"
>
> "That were impossible," returned the young man; "he called you by a thousand endearing epithets, that I may not presume to use, but to the justice of which I can warmly testify. Once, indeed, he said – "
>
> Duncan ceased speaking; for while his eyes were riveted on those of Alice, who had turned towards him with the eagerness of filial affection, the same strong, horrid cry, as before, filled the air, and rendered him mute. (p. 61)

> "[T]o heaven will I return my thanks!" exclaimed the younger sister, rising from the encircling arms of Cora, and casting herself, with enthusiastic gratitude, on the naked rock; "to that heaven who has spared the tears of a gray-headed father; has saved the lives of those I so much love – "
>
> Both Heyward, and the more tempered Cora, witnessed the act of involuntary emotion with powerful sympathy, the former secretly believing that piety had never worn a form so lovely, as it had now assumed in the youthful person of Alice. Her eyes were radiant with the glow of grateful feelings; the flush of her beauty was again seated on her cheeks, and her whole soul seemed ready and anxious to pour out its thanksgivings, through the medium of her eloquent features. But when her lips moved, the words they should have uttered appeared frozen by some new and sudden chill. Her bloom gave place to the paleness of death; her soft and melting eyes grew hard, and seemed contracting with horror; while those hands, which she had raised, clasped in each other, towards heaven, dropped in horizontal lines before her, the fingers pointing forward

in convulsed motion. Heyward turned the instant she gave a direction to his suspicions, and, peering just above the ledge which formed the threshold of the open outlet of the cavern, he beheld the malignant, fierce, and savage features of le Renard Subtil. (p. 87)

In both these passages, the mannerly illusion arises from the language of domestic affection in which Cooper's characters seem bent on conversing. It is a language that in some sense secures the world for them, for its epistemic style amounts to what I would call an ideological "settlement" of reality. There is nothing wild in this language, and not entirely (indeed, if at all) because Cooper is endorsing the vision of life implicit in the words. To the contrary, he seems intent on attenuating the language (as with Duncan's "thousand endearing epithets") until, like drawn gold, by its own fineness it seems about to break. But it does not just come apart. It is interrupted instead: first by the repetition of the mysterious "horrid cry" the wanderers have heard before, then by the interposition of Magua's fierce visage between Alice and the world just as she is about to pray, an interposition Cooper nicely reflects back to Heyward so as to have him (much as do his readers later during the massacre) know horror without directly knowing, at first, at any rate, its cause. Her fear becomes his anxiety. For her part, Alice is not just rendered innocently speechless. She is transformed by what confronts her; her imminent prayer is replaced by a chill silence that makes her look like a wholly different figure. This is her sudden Americanization.

Throughout the novel, Cooper pushes his two languages together; where the codes meet is his frontier, a domain characterized by the linked opposites that Cooper saw as marking the dialectic of American space.[25] In his preface to the first edition of *The Spy,* Cooper ridiculed Brockden Brown for yoking opposites in the "cave scene" of Brown's wilderness novel, where, as Cooper put it, we find "an American, a savage, a wild cat, and a tomahawk, in a conjunction that never did, nor ever will occur."[26] Brown, however, as Cooper's tone might suggest, was as much Cooper's model as Cooper was to be Mark Twain's. As Brown's hero falls asleep in the orderly world of a settled landscape, only to wake up disoriented, inexplicably lost in the wilderness, so Cooper's wanderers in *The Last of the Mohicans* wake from the sleep of their culture to find themselves exposed, in the wilderness of his words, to the deracinations of a landscape from which almost every sort of order – indeed, even their own lives, as it seems again and again, and the very words on their lips – appears to have been erased.

As Brown found the wilderness within his character's (and his own) mind, so Cooper found it not in the lateral expanses of American space but in his own capacity for violence, his own sense that the American text was a frail pretense written over both the continent and the consciousness. Perhaps as "the Last of the Coopers"[27] he saw in the dispossession of the Indians, as other critics have suggested, some expression of his family's sad losses, losses that must have enraged him. Perhaps his imagination, below the level of conscious control, found in the historically accurate violence of the New York border a vehicle of revenge against a nation whose myths no longer, deep inside in his private sense of things, seemed his own. If he erased the marks of possession from the land and joined with some energy in the assaults launched in this novel against the innocent representatives of polite social order, it was because the incendiary's role – indeed, that of the savage warrior – allowed him to indulge powerful emotions that he probably neither understood nor could otherwise control. It is no secret that his conscious relation to the American public was a difficult one, especially in the second and third decades of his career. To see that same difficulty at work in his invention of the wilderness in his first border romance is to understand how complicated his unconscious imaginative allegiances were in that book and, by extension, throughout his career. The very terms in which he cast his American tales show his face, like Alice's, capable of remarkable transformations. Indeed, one sometimes feels in reading Cooper much as Heyward does as he watches Alice's sweet face washed with horror, and then, following her clue, discovers Magua's rough visage right behind him. One feels, that is, that some vision of piety is suddenly replaced by the "malignant, fierce, and savage features" of a quite different (albeit in Cooper's own case a related) being. Cooper never showed himself particularly capable of making pious prayers, as Alice was about to do before that other face suddenly came so close to her. He could, and did, however, assume that "malignant" mask that cowed her. Wearing it, as so many characters in this novel wear their own wild disguises, he could find himself *in* the wilderness much as, in writing the book, he ultimately found the wilderness in his language, in himself.

NOTES

1. Wayne Franklin, *The New World of James Fenimore Cooper* (Chicago: University of Chicago Press, 1982), esp. pp. 75–118.

2. That "the neutral ground" is far from the wilderness Cooper later was to explore is confirmed by the fact that the term itself appears only once, by my count, in the first edition of *The Spy*. When Frances Wharton is climbing the mountain late in the novel, in search of her brother and Harvey Birch, she comes upon a farm whose owner — either because of the war or the sterility of the soil — has been "compelled to abandon the advantages that he had obtained over the wilderness" (*The Spy: A Tale of the Neutral Ground*, ed. James H. Pickering [Schenectady: New College & University Press, 1971], p. 379).

3. *The Spy*, pp. 313–14.

4. In *The Spy*, for instance, the journey of Frances Wharton up the mountain brings her into uncertain, potentially dangerous terrain. But Frances is allowed to turn and glance back at the valley, where a glimpse of her customary world reassures her. It is precisely this kind of backward glance which seems impossible for the characters of *The Last of the Mohicans*.

5. See Franklin, pp. 218–21, 245, for a more extended discussion of "centers" and "edges" in Cooper.

6. On this entanglement of Cooper's own imagination with the wilderness in this novel, see my discussion of the "Glenn's" episode in *The New World of James Fenimore Cooper*, pp. 233–5, 245–8.

7. James Fenimore Cooper [grandson], *The Legends and Traditions of a Northern County* (New York: G. P. Putnam's Sons, 1921), p. 171.

8. See J. H. French, *Gazetteer of the State of New York* (Syracuse: R. Pearsall Smith, 1860), pp. 150–1.

9. See Cooper's letter of March 1842 to *Brother Jonathan*, in James F. Beard, ed., *Letters and Journals of James Fenimore Cooper* (Cambridge: Harvard University Press, 1960–68), 4:252. Cooper's disclaimer here is part of a complicated attempt to keep *The Pioneers* free from his

current public wrangles. For the context of his remarks about "new country," see *The New World of James Fenimore Cooper*, pp. 78–9.

10. Between 1800 and 1810, the decade during which Cooper spent three years there, Oswego County experienced precisely the rapid kind of population growth that Cooper's home county of Otsego had experienced one decade earlier. So perhaps he was right, perhaps he indeed recovered on the shores of Ontario some glimpse of what he had been too young to see near Cooperstown in the early 1790s. See French, *Gazetteer*, p. 151, for comparative population figures.

11. *Letters and Journals* 1:10. See 1:12 for other rumors passed on by Cooper.

12. Ibid. On the embargo, see Beard's note, 1:11.

13. Ibid., 1:11.

14. Ibid., 1:128. In her *Pages and Pictures from the Writings of James Fenimore Cooper* (1860; rpt. Secaucus, N.J.: Castle Books, 1980), the novelist's daughter Susan claimed that it was one of the Englishmen who suggested to Cooper the idea of using this setting. She also wrote that Cooper had "examined closely" the vicinity of the falls at the time, "with a view to accurate description at a later hour" (p. 146).

15. Timothy Dwight, *Travels in New England and New York* (1821–22), ed. Barbara Miller Solomon (Cambridge: Harvard University Press, 1969), 2:163.

16. Ibid., 3:288.

17. Ibid., 3:288–9.

18. Ibid., 3:287–8.

19. Quoted in James Austin Holden, "*The Last of the Mohicans*, Cooper's Historical Inventions, and His Cave," New York State Historical Association *Proceedings* 16(1917): 244–5. Holden provides a very full background for Cooper's use of the Glens Falls setting in the novel.

20. Dwight, *Travels*, 2:406.

21. Compare the women's "curiosity" with Harvey Birch's "unconquerable desire" to watch as the Skinner who has been hanged kicks about in the deserted barn. Cooper later says that Harvey "continued gazing on this scene with a kind of infatuation" even after the traitor had become "a hideous, livid corpse" (*The Spy*, pp. 408–9).

22. On the bloodiness of this book, see Thomas Philbrick, "*The Last of the Mohicans* and the Sounds of Discord," *American Literature*, 43(1971): 29.

23. Terence Martin, "From the Ruins of History: *The Last of the Mohicans*," *Novel: A Forum on Fiction*, 2(1969): 221. Martin further argues that Cooper was naively attempting to portray "civilization meeting sav-

agism along its frontiers" (p. 223), that "the forces of savagery" were "the ultimate enemy" (p. 223), and that civilization represented for Cooper a "ponderous but commendable work," unquestionably worth defense (p. 225). As I go on to say, however, parts of Cooper's imagination were on each side of the battle. In no way was he merely defensive of civilization or merely appalled by "savagery." Those were simply the surface categories of his plot.

24. See Philbrick, "The Sounds of Discord."
25. See *The New World of James Fenimore Cooper,* pp. 57–61, 214–16.
26. *The Spy,* p. 31.
27. When Cooper's father, Judge William Cooper, died in 1809, he left sizable fortunes to each of his five sons. James, the youngest of them, was the only one left alive by 1820, and by then the family's wealth was substantially gone. Because he lost control of the family's mansion in Cooperstown as well as his own new, unfinished house there, Cooper had been virtually dispossessed from the world of his youth, the "Woods" in which, so said his sister Hannah, he and the now dead brothers had been "bred." Surely some part of Chingachgook's and Uncas's woe was his own. On this question, see James F. Beard's brief suggestion in his introduction to the novel (p. xxx) and H. Daniel Peck's more extensive discussion in *A World by Itself: The Pastoral Moment in Cooper's Fiction* (New Haven: Yale University Press, 1977), pp. 141–5.

From Atrocity to Requiem: History in *The Last of the Mohicans*

TERENCE MARTIN

*T*HE *Last of the Mohicans* is the bloodiest and most troubling of Cooper's five Leatherstocking novels. In this second novel of what was not yet conceived as a series, Cooper moves with ponderous insistence toward a vision of history that includes both the savagery of fact and the tragedy of inexorable process. The Massacre at Fort William Henry midway in the narrative and the death of Uncas at the end stand as climactic points of reference in a world of mayhem and disorder; juxtaposed in Cooper's imagination, they engage issues of civilization and progress that were of fundamental importance to a colonial society waging war on its frontiers. The dominating irony of *Mohicans,* the unsettling revelation of the tale, is that the codes of conduct melting away during the atrocities at Fort William Henry belong to the same civilizing impulse, the same set of values, the same agenda, that make the death of Uncas inevitable.

That civilization can appear both commendable and destructive in the same novel should not be surprising when we consider the attitudes expressed in much of Cooper's fiction. As Roy Harvey Pearce and Henry Nash Smith have pointed out in seminal discussions of American literature and the frontier, Cooper was ambivalent about the westering advance of the society to which he belonged: because it was the vehicle of acknowledged cultural values (embodied in religion, science, and the arts), the advance was beneficial; to the extent that it spawned waste and devastation out of a disregard for the pristine qualities of nature, it was regrettable.[1] Not only is Natty Bumppo suspicious of settlements and their twisty ways throughout the Leatherstocking novels. Not only does he bemoan the community's bacchanalian attacks on natural resources in *The Pioneers* (1823). As Hawk-eye in *The Last of the Mohicans*, he formulates the principle that "'natur is sadly abused'" by civilized men, once they get "'the mastery'" (p. 121). With *mastery* (the persistent goal of the whites) comes *abuse* – portentous, threatening, unpredictably at odds with the environment that nourishes the native inhabitants.

Cooper is far from alone in dramatizing the profound difference between civilized and native attitudes toward nature. In "Chocorura's Curse" (1830), his contemporary Lydia Maria Child focuses on the consequences of this difference: When an unsuspecting Indian boy dies from poison set out for a fox which had long annoyed a group of settlers, the result is escalating vengeance. A century later, in the quieter world of *Death Comes for the Archbishop*, Willa Cather articulates with benign clarity what had become a familiar distinction. Traveling with his Indian friend Eusabio is for Bishop Latour "like travelling with the landscape made human." The white man's way, Latour realizes, is "to assert himself" in any environment, "to change it, make it over a little (at least to leave some mark or memorial of his sojourn)." The native way, on the contrary, is to pass through a country "and leave no trace, like fish through the water, or birds through the air."[2] Such an impressive harmony with nature has nourished life, both physical and spiritual, "from immemorial times."

The immediate situation in *The Last of the Mohicans* goes far beyond any manifestation of harmony or habit of making the environment "over a little." The bewildering intensity of war, as Cooper writes, "had armed friend against friend, and brought natural enemies to combat by each other's side" (p. 198). Tribes now fight related tribes in a hopeless confusion of loyalties. Heightened by violence on a scale unique to Cooper and other writers of the period, policies of *mastery* and *abuse* generate in *The Last of the Mohicans* an intensifying world of chaos. When Duncan Heyward asks Hawk-eye about the cause of the frightful disorder around them, Cooper's scout replies that the explanation would be "'long and melancholy.'" But one thing, as he says, is clear: "'the evil has been mainly done by men with white skins'" (p. 227).

Cooper brings recorded fact and relentless process into dramatic focus by means of plot, characterization, and, most important, setting. At the outset he makes us aware that European motives and animosities are responsible for the action of his "Narrative of 1757," that in this North American theater of the Seven Years War between England and France opposing forces had to battle the wilderness (frequently for months) before they could get close enough to kill each other. Nature, Cooper is at sardonic pains to tell us, provided wide and almost impenetrable boundaries between the colonies of France and England. The feverish motives of men, however, overcame every difficulty; eventually there were no wilderness barriers or dark and secret places in the woods that could "claim exemption from the inroads of those who had pledged their blood to satiate their vengeance, or to uphold the cold and selfish policy of the distant monarchs of Europe" (p. 11). A European war has come to the American wilderness; once arrived, it has combined with native forces and become something different, something hybrid, alien, no longer European, something subversive of civilized values.

Having set a general context for his narrative, Cooper singles out the locale of *The Last of the Mohicans* by telling us that no area was more beset with "the cruelty and fierceness" of "savage warfare" (p. 11). And he sees to it that the action of his novel bears out this contention. Repeatedly, he stresses the importance of the wilderness in shaping the course and conduct of battle. Recurrent metaphors of burial and of being swallowed by the forest emphasize the voraciousness and primal strength of nature. Of necessity in this fearsome world, Hawk-eye and his party contribute to the violence: When a wounded foal threatens to betray their position, Chingachgook instantly slashes its throat and casts it into the river, where it bobs downstream "gasping audibly for breath with its ebbing life." It is, Cooper writes, a "deed of apparent cruelty, but of real necessity," an act betokening the resolve necessary for survival (p. 47). A short while later, during a fierce skirmish with the Hurons (in which Duncan Heyward arms himself with a tomahawk), three resolute comrades dispatch an enemy in a single instant: "the tomahawk of Heyward, and the rifle of Hawk-eye, descended on the skull of the Huron, at the same moment that the knife of Uncas reached his heart" (p. 113).

Constantly verging toward excess, the violence of *The Last of the*

Mohicans frequently swirls around the figure of Hawk-eye and threatens to transform him from scout to savage. At the end of a fierce battle with a band of Hurons, Chingachgook and Magua roll on the ground in furious combat until the Mohican thrusts with his knife and Magua falls back as if dead. As Chingachgook leaps to his feet with a shout of triumph, Hawk-eye raises his rifle butt high in the air to strike "'a finishing blow'" that will not rob Chingachgook "'of his right to the scalp!'" Magua's athletic escape chagrins Hawk-eye and stirs him to make sure the other enemy bodies are in fact dead. He moves over the scene of battle stabbing the dead Hurons "with as much coolness, as though they had been so many brute carcasses," even though Chingachgook, with an instinct for honor, has "already torn the emblems of victory from the unresisting heads of the slain" (p. 114). It is an appalling spectacle to contemplate – that of Hawk-eye, Natty Bumppo, "the honest, but implacable scout," stabbing the corpses of scalped men – generating a sense of surfeit because Natty is completing a completed act. A motive of prudence, of course, dictates his actions and perhaps mitigates their brutality. But mutilating corpses is hardly what we expect from Cooper's figure of Leatherstocking.

H. Daniel Peck points out that in significant ways Hawk-eye "stands outside" the developing drama of *The Last of the Mohicans*, commenting and guiding, to be sure, serving as valuable liaison between red world and white, but, given the structure of the novel, never becoming a figure with personal commitment, never discerning a geography of fulfillment.[3] It is a provocative observation, not only for Peck's idea of a double quest in *The Last of the Mohicans* (that of Heyward and that of Uncas), but for our understanding of Natty Bumppo as a character who developed in Cooper's imagination over a period of years. Let us recall that Natty was born into fiction at the age of three-score and ten in *The Pioneers*, a snaggle-toothed hunter who contributes irregularly to the issues of a novel in which authority and order emanate from Judge Temple as father-figure. *The Last of the Mohicans* makes him much younger, a scout famed for his prowess as a marksman. In *The Prairie* (1827) Cooper staged Natty's death far to the west of the hunter's familiar terrain, even as he planned that novel to be the conclusion of a three-part series. Writing to the publishing firm of Carey and Lea in October 1826, he announced that "Pioneers, Mohicans, and this book will form a connected series, which will do to print and sell separately." In the same month he advised his British publisher that *The Pioneers, The Last of the Mohicans,* and *The Prairie* "will form a complete series of tales."[4]

As a novel designed to complete a series, *The Prairie* moves Natty Bumppo center stage for the first time and – going further – reconstitutes the earlier tales in his image with an insistent strategy of allusion. Duncan Middleton, for example, virtually brings *The Last of the Mohicans* onto the prairie with him. During the cumbersome recognition scene in Chapter 10, Middleton discloses that he is the grandson of Duncan Heyward, that his middle name is Uncas, and that he has a brother and two cousins named Nathaniel. Such evidence of pride in the past not only unlocks Natty Bumppo's memories but ratifies them socially. When an ebullient Natty later indulges in a host of recollections involving episodes in *The Last of the Mohicans,* Middleton recognizes them all, and Cooper – connecting his series with vengeance – tells us in a footnote that those "who have read the preceding books . . . will readily understand the allusions."[5]

References to *The Pioneers* are different in kind but no less important. The Natty Bumppo who speaks of his experience in a courtroom and in the stocks is still perplexed by it and very much aware of his shame. His account of why he came to the prairie, fashioned for the ears of Mahtoree, provides a synoptic interpretation of his life. He had passed most of his early days in the forest, he says, happy and close to his Creator, "'But the axes of the choppers awoke me.'" Only when the death of Major Effingham released him from an old commitment could he "'get beyond the accursed sounds.'" He has come to the prairie "'to escape the wasteful temper of my people.'"[6] With its abuse of nature and sounds of settlement, Templeton continues to burden Natty Bumppo's consciousness. One happy memory remains, however: When the dying Natty asks Middleton to send his rifle to one who lives in the Otsego hills, his love for Oliver Effingham becomes part of the reverie of his final hours. And once Natty sees the noble Hard-Heart as another version of Uncas, the bequest of *The Last of the Mohicans* to *The Prairie* is complete. Middleton/Heyward and Hard-

Heart/Uncas can stand on either side of the dying Natty with cumulative effect.

By levying on the earlier novels with revisionist purpose, *The Prairie* not only augments its status as a book which "closes the career" of Leatherstocking but demonstrates the assurance Cooper had acquired in defining his character. When he resurrected Natty Bumppo in *The Pathfinder* (1840) and (at his youngest) in *The Deerslayer* (1841), Cooper continued to shape him with authority and purpose into a classic image of the noble frontiersman, an enduring character whom Walt Whitman described as existing "from everlasting to everlasting."[7] In *The Last of the Mohicans,* however, we encounter an anomalous and unfinished Natty Bumppo. Not having conceived him as the touchstone of a series (either of three parts or five), Cooper seems unsure what to do with a lethal Hawk-eye in a war-stricken wilderness, unsure (until the end) of how he relates to history and to his Mohican friends. To be sure, Hawk-eye asserts that he is "'genuine white'" (p. 31), invokes his distinction between the "gifts" of a white man and those of an Indian, and takes the daughters of Major Munro under his stern protection. Still, *The Last of the Mohicans* remains surprising and disturbing in its presentation of Natty Bumppo. Not only does he stab dead bodies and rush into battle yelling "'Exterminate the varlets!'" (p. 11), but he tells Duncan Heyward that "'to outwit the knaves it is lawful to practise things, that may not be naturally the gift of a white skin'" (p. 229). And to David Gamut he admits that it is hard to deal with an Indian as "'you would with a fellow christian'" (p. 274).

The violence and chaos of *The Last of the Mohicans,* as we shall see, threaten to blur a necessary distinction between Natty Bumppo and Chingachgook by implicating the scout in actions Cooper would come to deplore. More carefully worked out, the later appearances of the two characters in *The Pathfinder* and *The Deerslayer* present a more adamic Natty and a more obedient Serpent. In *The Pathfinder,* for example, Natty says that "'peace and marcy'" rather than "'bloodshed and warfare'" are his "'real gifts'"; as a white man, he says, he "'cannot mangle a dead enemy.'" In *The Deerslayer,* he is described as "guileless" and sincere. Chingachgook, patient and helpful in *The Pathfinder,* becomes "an Apollo of the wilderness" in *The Deerslayer*. Natty, in other words, remains not only pure but aware of his purity in the final novels of the series, a character released from the burdens of experience, a frontiersman ruled by his conscience to whom truth is a "polar star."[8] But in *The Last of the Mohicans* his character is still in the making, at times violent, at times aloof, at times almost soured by life. And Chingachgook is the canny and ferocious Great Serpent of the Mohicans, who lies coiled on the warpath and strikes terror in the hearts of his enemies.

The accumulating violence of *Mohicans* reaches its apex in the Massacre at Fort William Henry. With the French and Indian troops standing by, the conquered British soldiers march from the Fort, followed by the women and children. Montcalm has granted the English an honorable surrender, and the soldiers of France know how to respect its terms. Not so their Indian allies, who place no value on a tactical victory. Aflame with a desire for battle, an Indian precipitates an incident that leads to the general massacre. Flourishing tomahawks and knives, the Indians descend upon their victims, converting formal surrender to a scene of bloody triumph and abject terror. An Indian catches an infant by the feet, whirls it high in the air, explodes its head against a rock, then kills the distraught mother. Amid the chaos and cruelty, Cooper's Hurons kneel and drink the blood of their victims as it flows in rivulets along the earth. With the rules of civilized warfare completely broken down, the scene becomes a carnival of atrocity, dominated by cruelty and savage violence.

Graphic as it is, Cooper's account of the Massacre seems not to have been exaggerated. Contemporary versions of what happened attest to the butchery and may well have provided details for Cooper's presentation. Jonathan Carver, for example, reported as an eyewitness that while the garrison (along with women and children) were assembled for surrender, a large number of Indians began to plunder, "to attack the sick and wounded," and, finally, "to murder those that were nearest to them without any distinction." Carver almost despaired of giving "any tolerable idea of the horrid scene that now ensued; men, women, and children were dispatched in the most wanton and cruel manner, and immediately scalped. Many of these savages drank the blood of their victims, as it flowed warm from the fatal wound." To make matters more appalling, he "could plainly perceive the French officers walking about at some distance, discoursing together with apparent unconcern." A concise story in the *New-York Mercury* (on August 22, 1757) was even gorier in telling readers that "the Throats of most, if not all the Women, were cut, their Bellies riped [sic] open, their Bowels torn out, and thrown upon the Faces of their dead and dying Bodies; and 'tis said that all the Women were murdered one Way or other. That the Children were taken by the Heels, and their Brains beat out against the Trees and Stones, and not one of them saved." It is no wonder that Jonathan Carver thought the carnage was "not to be paralleled in modern history."[9]

In presenting the Massacre at Fort William Henry, Cooper explicitly adopts the role of historian, to the extent that he later feels the need of retiring from Clio's "sacred precincts" to the "proper limits of our own vocation" (p. 180). What characterizes the event for him is that it happened, that it is a specific recorded event, verifiable, documented, different in kind from and more appalling than anything else in his novel. Philip Roth once spoke of the burden on the writer in the twentieth century when actual events frequently beggar the imagination, when everyday headlines carry stories more bizarre than one finds in fiction. Cooper encounters this problem in *The Last of the Mohicans*. He has directed his "Narrative of 1757" to a day in August when what happened at Fort William Henry outdistances his fiction. So dominant is this moment of history that it totally obscures his primary characters, even as it raises a question of moral responsibility that reaches deep into the moral fabric of the novel.

At this point in his narrative, Cooper confronts one of the basic problems of the historical novelist – how to handle fictional characters when dramatizing episodes of history – and resolves it by dismissing them in the order of their importance. Through Heyward's eyes, we see Hawk-eye, a prisoner, being led toward the Fort with his arms tied behind him, his face "haggard and careworn, and his air dejected, as though he felt the deepest degradation at having fallen into the power of his enemies" (p. 148). In a literal sense, Hawk-eye is the prisoner of the French (though how he was captured we never learn). In a larger sense, however, he is the prisoner of history, more specifically, of a historical event, a fictional character made impotent by circumstances in which he has no part. If he stands outside the developing drama throughout much of the novel, he is helplessly eclipsed at this specific point. With Uncas and Chingachgook, the removal is absolute: During the massacre they drop completely out of the novel. Cooper does not subordinate these three characters; he dismisses them. They make no exit from the stage they have occupied so consistently; they simply vanish.

Although Cooper frequently places his characters against a generalized historical backdrop, he shies away from involving them in specific historical events. They are, in a sense, *of* history without being *in* it. It is obvious that he does not want Natty Bumppo and the Mohicans present at the time of the Massacre. Not only do they lack historical existence, but the imaginative conception that brings them into being gives them such force and vitality that they always have an impact on the circumstances around them. Though they could hardly turn the tide of battle outside Fort William Henry, the presence of Natty, Uncas, and Chingachgook might force Cooper to qualify his presentation of the Massacre. Even Heyward and Major Munro, less powerfully conceived, lose their identity as characters during the scene outside the Fort. The more passive characters (Cora, Alice, David Gamut) remain briefly and afford a point of view from which to describe the action, until they, too, are withdrawn, leaving Cooper free to castigate Montcalm for "an apathy which has never been explained" before resuming his story (p. 179).

As we know, Cooper implicates Montcalm deeply in the Massacre. According to Cooper's traditional if sometimes ambivalent vision of history and progress, the Huron allies of the French exemplify the wild and savage violence that Montcalm's and Cooper's civilization has supposedly grown beyond, that it has harnessed, repressed, or made latent by such self-protective rules of warfare as an honorable and formal surrender. When such violence is unleashed, Montcalm stands by, a spectator to the massacre, Cooper blames him as if he were participating in the atrocity. And of course Montcalm is participating: He has allied himself with savage forces, against which, when they erupt, the forms of civilization (including his role as military commander) are helpless and meaningless.

Other commentators, we might note, were even harsher on Montcalm. Timothy Dwight, for example, doubled his censure of the French general by recalling in detail his similar conduct at Fort Oswego the previous year, when he had "violated the conditions" of surrender and permitted his Indian allies to "rob the garrison, massacre several of the men on parade," then to "scalp all the sick in the hospital." The *New-York Mercury* similarly reminded its readers of the French "perfidy" at Oswego the year before as a way of heightening its criticism of Montcalm.[10]

Cooper folds his awareness of what he calls the "horrid scene" at Oswego into the brooding consciousness of Montcalm as a way of exploring a principle of moral responsibility at the center of the issue. In taking savage allies that one cannot, at crucial moments, control, one risks, almost invites, ruthless measures of warfare. Since the Indians have their own code of battle, to join with them against a common enemy is to become a party to the result. To hope for the best, to hope that they will, in civilized terms, behave themselves, is at best self-delusion, at worst hypocrisy. Thus Cooper implicates Montcalm in the Massacre even as he makes him unhappily aware of his part in the potential catastrophe. During a peace talk Montcalm has mentioned his Huron allies to Duncan Heyward, saying, "'I find it difficult, even now, to limit them to the usages of war'" (p. 154). Meant as a warning to force the British to an early surrender, the remark also serves as an admission of limited authority. It is a confidence from one civilized man to another that danger is to be apprehended from the forces of savagery – the ultimate enemy. On the night before the battle Montcalm muses over the "deep responsibility they assume, who disregard the means to attain their end," and of the danger of unleashing forces "which it exceeds human power to control" (pp. 170–1). At this moment he is a troubled human being, divided in commitment, unsure of what he should do. But he shakes off such reflections as signs of weakness at a time demanding resolve and takes no steps to avert the impending disaster.

The implications of the problem of moral responsibility in the making of history are by no means limited to Montcalm's conduct at Fort William Henry, though Cooper nowhere else speaks so directly to the point. The five Leatherstocking novels repeatedly advance a simple notion of cultural relativism, most often when the ingenuous Natty Bumppo asserts his whiteness even as he accounts for Indian methods of warfare. What is right for an Indian, Natty believes, is wrong for a white man. In *The Pathfinder*, one finds an excellent example of Natty's thinking when he speaks of the hardest temptation he ever had to overcome. During wartime, as he tells the story (it is the same war that we see in *The Last of the Mohicans*, though at a different time and place), he had come upon six Mingoes, enemy Indians, sleeping beside the trail, their rifles and powder horns piled to one side. "'What an opportunity that would have been for the Sarpent,'" he muses, "'lives and scalps for the taking.'" For Natty, however, it was "'a desperate trial.'" Unable as a white man to kill – let alone scalp – the Mingoes, unwilling even to take their rifles because "'a white man can no more attack an unarmed man than a sleeping inimy,'" he later ambushed the party, dispatching five of the six. (Ambushes, he tells us, are lawful in wartime.) "'Luckily,'" he says, Chingachgook was following not far behind, and when the Serpent appeared, the five Mingo scalps were at his belt, "'hanging where they ought to be.'" "'So, you see,'" concludes the storyteller, "'nothing was lost by doing right, either in the way of honor or in that of profit.'"[11]

The events of this remarkable homily obviously inform the idea of racial "gifts" that Cooper is at increasing pains to articulate as the Leatherstocking tales take shape. What is right for an Indian, Natty Bumppo believes, may be wrong for a white man. As he says in the same novel, his law is "'to fight always like a white man and never like an Injin'"; Chingachgook "'has his fashions, and I have mine; and yet we have fou't, side by side, these many years, without either's thinking a hard thought consarning the other's ways.'" But this is Natty speaking fourteen years after *Mohicans*, at a time when Cooper had committed himself to develop his frontiersman's innocence. It is in *The Pathfinder*, after all, that one finds the wondrously qualified definition of Natty as "a sort of type of what Adam might have been supposed to be before the fall, though certainly not without sin."[12] In *The Last of the Mohicans*, however, the relationship between Natty and Chingachgook is still in the making, and the thrust of Cooper's narrative makes it clear that Natty's notion of "gifts," later so useful, can seem inadequate when the problem of responsibility for the acts of Indian allies is brought explicitly to the fore.

When Natty Bumppo and his party are making their way toward Fort William Henry, to take the most provocative example offered by the narrative, they are challenged in the darkness by a young French sentry. Answering in French, Duncan Heyward succeeds in fooling the sentry into thinking he is a French officer who has captured the daughters of Major Munro and is taking them to Montcalm. The young Frenchman gallantly assures the young women of Montcalm's hospitality, wishes them well, hears the voice of Cora saying "'Adieu, mon ami'" and that of Heyward adding "'bonne nuit, mon comarade,'" then hums a lively tune to himself as the party steals away. A moment later, Natty and Heyward pull up short at the sound of "a long and heavy groan," then another, fainter, and notice that Chingachgook is missing from their group. While they hesitate in indecision, the Great Serpent of his tribe glides out of a thicket and rejoins them: "with one hand he attached the reeking scalp of the unfortunate young Frenchman to his girdle, and with the other he replaced the knife and tomahawk that had drunk his blood. He then took his wonted station, with the air of a man who believed he had done a deed of merit" (pp. 137–8).

The sudden and shocking nature of the deed has its effect on Natty Bumppo – and perhaps even more so on the reader, who has, for one thing, been told earlier that Chingachgook's tomahawk and scalping knife were "of English manufacture," savage weapons made by a civilized nation (p. 29). Leaning on his rifle, Natty muses "in profound silence." Then shaking his head sadly, he mutters (in a virtual soliloquy), "'Twould have been a cruel and an unhuman act for a white-skin; but 'tis the gift and natur of an Indian, and I suppose it should not be denied! I could wish, though, it had befallen an accursed Mingo, rather than that gay, young boy, from the old countries!'" (p. 138). Somehow, this momentary sadness and matter-of-fact explanation seem inadequate. For in presenting the incident Cooper has spoken to the reader in a language Natty admittedly does not understand and included the well-meaning sentry in a tacit bond of civility: Heyward has twice called him "comrade," Cora has called him "friend," both terms part of the deception, to be sure, but both without rancor or malicious intent. Suddenly the sentry seems kind, generous, and very civilized, and Chingachgook's deed proves not only embarrassing but alien in its claim to "merit." Conquering his disgust out of a concern to keep the sisters from realizing what has occurred, Heyward responds abruptly by saying the deed is done, over, "'and though better it were left undone, cannot be amended'"; after asking how they might proceed, he rejects Hawk-eye's idea (offered with reluctance) that "'by sending the Mohicans in front, we might then cut a lane through [the French] sentries, and enter the fort over the dead bodies'" (p. 138). One French sentry is unfortunately dead but with his little group in a tight squeeze, Hawk-eye hopes the Mohicans might helpfully eliminate others.

Cooper's handling of this incident suggests the dangers inherent in taking savage allies and prefigures the larger action – the moment of actual history – from which Natty Bumppo is excluded. Indeed, it is a cameo version of the Massacre at Fort William Henry, featuring Natty and Chingachgook as partners, with Heyward in the role of civilized participant-audience. The killing of the French sentry strikes a disturbing note at the moral center of the novel, for Chingachgook is the trusted friend of Natty Bumppo and the father of Uncas. In any struggle involving life and death in the wilderness one feels able to count on this warrior of experience and bravery, wisdom and craft, and, indeed, one can. Yet when Chingachgook perpetrates a shocking deed of valor, Natty can do nothing about it except to wish that the victim had been an enemy Indian. There is no ground for a reprimand; there is no hope of change. To fight alongside Chingachgook, to accept him as a partner, is, inevitably, to risk involvement in this kind of incident. Just as Montcalm is implicated in the actions of his Indian allies, so is Natty Bumppo implicated in the action of Chingachgook. The figure from history and the imaginary character bear a subtle relationship that Cooper does not otherwise stress – he could hardly have had Montcalm use the idea of *gifts* to rationalize the Massacre at William Henry any more than he could afford to castigate Natty for allying himself with the Serpent. By stressing the Massacre, however, he has blamed Montcalm for a kind of liaison to which Natty Bumppo is deeply committed.

The depth of Cooper's distress over the Massacre comes ultimately, I believe, from his sense that civilization as he knows and respects it is crumbling, withering, outside Fort William Henry, that the forces of atrocity, in some nightmarish way, are destroying in a moment the ponderous and commendable work of centuries. By showing that Natty Bumppo likewise puts civilized deportment at risk, Cooper adds to the sense of hazard and perhaps builds better than he knows by suggesting that the agent of atrocity may be a permanent part of one's life. For in bringing Cooper's concern into the modern world such writers as Joseph Conrad and Philip Caputo take it one frightening step further out of their conviction that we need a network of civilized codes and standards, assumptions and restraints (the very things Montcalm abjured), if we are not to succumb to our own potential for barbarism.

In the Prologue to *A Rumor of War*, for example, Caputo defines both the kind of war fought in Vietnam and his sense of the individual as a social and ethical human being in that war. By telling us that "there were no Normandies or Gettysburgs" or "epic clashes" in Vietnam, he distinguishes the fighting from battles honored in history. Continuing with deeper import, he sketches a world of frightening unfamiliarity "out where we were," a world with "no churches, no police, no laws, no newspapers, or any of the restraining influences without which the earth's population of virtuous people would be reduced by ninety-five percent. It was the dawn of creation in the Indochina bush, an ethical as well as geographical wilderness." Without restraints and "sanctioned to kill . . . , we sank into a brutish state," which could be offset only by one's "inner moral values, the attribute that is called character." Those who lacked character "plunged all the way down," revealing an unsuspected "capacity for malice."[13] Troubling in its own day, the massacre at Fort William Henry continues to have its epiphanies.

Out of the insistent chaos of *The Last of the Mohicans* emerges the heroic figure of Uncas, whose death brings a devastating note of finality to the novel. "'My boy,'" Chingachgook says, "'is the last of the Mohicans'" (p. 33). As the last of a high race, a warrior whose purity of descent accounts for his dignity and bravery, Uncas exemplifies a principle of order in the midst of the wild disorder of this fictional world. His appearance before the aged Tamenund resolves all questions of friend and foe. As he does at various points in *The Last of the Mohicans*, Cooper makes use of a sudden revelation, this time the emblem of the turtle on Uncas's breast that proclaims his identity to an astonished band of Delaware warriors and takes Tamenund back in wonder to the days of tribal glory. "'Uncas, the child of Uncas, is found!'" exclaims the patriarch, collapsing four generations into two (p. 310). For Tamenund, the return of Uncas signifies the fulfillment of a cherished tradition. Acknowledging the dispossession of his tribe, he believes that the white man who entered the land from the east "'may yet go off at the setting sun!'" (p. 305). Uncas lives even more intently in the promise of the same tradition. According to his fathers (as he tells the assembled Delawares), the Delawares will return to the sea and take their lands again when the Manitou announces the proper time: "'Our eyes are on the rising, and not towards the setting sun!'" (p. 311). With ironic consistency Cooper gives Tamenund the final words of the novel. Having spanned in his own life the entire history of his tribe, the sage of the Mohicans understands the meaning of Uncas's death from a full and unique perspective. Yet he clings to a vision of the future now bereft of the hero who was to have brought it into being: "'The pale-faces are masters of the earth, and the time of the red-men has not yet come again'" (p. 350).

Uncas, we should note, is frequently exempt from much of the violence and ferocity that pervade the novel. After an early skirmish with the Hurons, Chingachgook glides silently about taking the scalps of the enemy dead. "But Uncas," writes Cooper, "denying his habits, we had almost said his nature, flew with instinctive delicacy, accompanied by Heyward, to the assistance of the females." The sight of Cora and Alice in each others' arms moves Heyward to manly tears; as for Uncas, he "stood fresh and blood-stained from the combat, a calm, and, apparently, an unmoved looker-on, it is true, but with eyes that had already lost their fierceness, and were beaming with a sympathy that elevated him far above the intelligence, and advanced him probably centuries before the practices of his nation" (pp. 114–15). What Cooper does virtually throughout *The Last of the Mohicans* is to bestow on Uncas some of the qualities of Duncan Heyward, officer of the King and civilized hero. So dedicated is he to making the young Mohican worthy of admiration that (as in the passage above) he sometimes praises Uncas at the expense of other Indians to make him almost a gentleman – a sure sign of Cooper's fundamental belief in the superiority of his own culture.

Uncas lacks nothing in the way of courage and an Indian thirst for battle. In the forest he repeatedly displays greater perception than either his father or Natty Bumppo; in battle he is energetic and fearless. Indeed, Cooper seizes every opportunity to make Uncas athletic and formidable when the lives of Cora and Alice are in peril. Prior to showing a sensitive concern for the young women following the skirmish mentioned above, he has been as-tonishingly active in defending them. "When Uncas had brained his first antagonist," Cooper writes, "he turned, like a hungry lion, to seek another." Seeing a Huron grab Cora, he bounds through the air, descends "in a ball . . . on the chest of his enemy," and knocks him "headlong and prostrate" (pp. 112–13). And Uncas does take a scalp. In the ruins of Fort William Henry, when a Huron shoots at Chingachgook from the dark, Uncas conquers the would-be assassin and returns to the campfire with a fresh scalp at his belt. We note, however, that Cora and Alice are not present at this scene and perceive further that Cooper never has Uncas scalp an enemy when the daughters of Major Munro are present. Uncas, the image of Indian nobility, is made an exception, a gentle as well as fierce and noble savage, to qualify him for his special place in the novel and in the world of Cooper's fiction. For Uncas, as we know, is attracted to Cora, whom he admires silently, courteously, and unmistakably. In attending to the young women (an excep-tional thing in itself), Uncas shows a preference for Cora; in the first rescue of Heyward's party he leaps instinctively to her as-sistance; during the final pursuit of Magua and Cora he bounds far ahead of Heyward and Natty Bumppo, impelled by a personal if otherwise unexpressed feeling. Uncas takes extreme risks on

Cora's account and finally dies in a frantic attempt to rescue her from the evil Magua, who has been transformed from a skulking outcast to an embodiment of the Prince of Darkness to qualify him for a final encounter with the tragic hero.

It is in relation to Uncas that Cora's Negro-ness has a definite function in *The Last of the Mohicans*. By making her not only the conventional dark woman but also the partly Negro woman, Cooper at once puts Cora within the range of Uncas's admiration and denies any future to the romance. He cannot conceive of a marriage between the daughter of Major Munro, no matter her background, and an Indian, no matter how noble. Conversely, since he has taken pains to portray the highborn Mohican as a young chief of unmixed blood, Cooper can hardly forsake the purity of the tribe. The racial barriers of his imagination thus block such a union in a double way. Cora is an extra heroine, fated for death, not marriage, provided, I believe, because of Uncas's heroic stature, made partly – but unrecognizably – Negro to placate the social requirements of Cooper's imagination. The numerous suggestions regarding the mutual admiration of Cora and Uncas are subdued, qualified by Uncas's reserved demeanor as well as by Cora's modesty, but they are nonetheless clear, and it is equally clear that Cora's ancestry makes the admiration possible.

Cooper inserts the story of Uncas and Cora adventitiously into the larger story of the Mohican tribe. The primary drama has its own coherence and autonomy: At a moment of apparent renewal, with their champion identified in the pride of his youth and their traditions apparently vindicated, the Mohicans see their claim on the future collapse forever. Cast against the background of American history with its westering bias, the Mohican dream of reclaiming lands in the East is futile and forlorn. Their vision is backward in time, to an original glory they believe will return. Embodying the idea of rejuvenation in the figure of Uncas, Cooper enlarges the importance of a single life – and of a single death. The resonance of the ending comes from a revelatory vision of history as cyclical that generates the hope of beginning again.

The sense of absolute finality at the funeral of Uncas understandably constitutes the most powerful effect in the novel. Perhaps, as Joel Porte suggests, Cooper patterned his concluding chapter after the funeral of Hector in *The Iliad*.[14] Be that as it may, the parallel Porte notes does obtain: As Hector's tragedy is that of Troy, the tragedy of Uncas is that of the Mohicans, the first tribe dispossessed by the policies of European settlement. At times clumsily, at times with purpose and power, Cooper has taken us in *The Last of the Mohicans* from one kind of history to another, from documented scenes of atrocity to an extended requiem for native Americans – a people "sadly abused" by white men, as Natty Bumppo observes, once they gained "the mastery" (p. 121). In the course of the action he has confronted issues of morality, race, and the inevitable cost of civilization that have resonance for the American (and human) experience both in his time and ours.

NOTES

1. Roy Harvey Pearce, "The Leatherstocking Tales Re-examined," *South Atlantic Quarterly,* 46 (1947), 524–36. Henry Nash Smith, *Virgin Land: The American West as Symbol and Myth* (Cambridge, Mass.: Harvard University Press, 1950), chap. 6, "Leatherstocking and the Problem of Social Order," pp. 59–70.
2. Willa Cather, *Death Comes for the Archbishop* (New York: Alfred A. Knopf, 1950), pp. 232–3. The quoted words in the following sentence are from p. 294.
3. H. Daniel Peck, *A World by Itself: The Pastoral Moment in Cooper's Fiction* (New Haven: Yale University Press, 1977), p. 140.
4. *The Letters and Journals of James Fenimore Cooper,* ed. James Franklin Beard, 6 vols. (Cambridge, Mass.: Belknap Press of Harvard University Press, 1960–68), I, 168; I, 167.
5. *The Prairie* (New York: Penguin Books, 1987), p. 233.
6. Ibid., p. 213.
7. Horace Traubel, *With Walt Whitman in Camden: March 28–July 14, 1888* (New York: Rowman and Littlefield, 1961), p. 454.
8. *The Pathfinder* (New York: Penguin Books, 1987), p. 96, p. 78. *The Deerslayer* (New York: Penguin Books, 1987), pp. 237, 545.
9. Quotations from Jonathan Carver's *Travels* and from the *New-York Mercury* are drawn from the "Explanatory Notes" by James A. Sappenfield and E. N. Feltskog in *The Last of the Mohicans* (Albany: State University of New York Press, 1983), pp. 355–59, 362. In "James Fenimore Cooper and Fort William Henry," *American Literature* 32

(1960): 28–38, David P. French suggests that a British officer named John Young may have been the real-life counterpart of Duncan Heyward. Thomas Philbrick supplies excellent information on the Fort and the massacre in "The Sources of Cooper's Knowledge of Fort William Henry," *American Literature* 36 (1964): 209–14; and in "*The Last of the Mohicans* and the Sounds of Discord," *American Literature* 43 (1971): 25–41.

10. "Explanatory Notes" to *Mohicans*, p. 362.
11. *The Pathfinder*, pp. 435–6.
12. Ibid., pp. 24, 134.
13. Philip Caputo, *A Rumor of War* (New York: Holt, Rinehart, and Winston, 1977), pp. xiii, xviii.
14. Joel Porte, *The Romance in America: Studies in Cooper, Poe, Hawthorne, Melville, and James* (Middletown, Conn.: Wesleyan University Press, 1969), p. 39.

4

How Men and Women
Wrote Indian Stories

NINA BAYM

THE so-called "Indian stories" popular during the 1820s were exciting adventure tales portraying white occupation of the continent as both inevitable and justified, even if it annihilated the Indians. Although depicting an occasional "noble savage" and praising Indians who befriended whites, the stories mainly saw Indians as unalterably hostile to whites, unwilling to coexist with or assimilate to white civilization. The narratives alleged that Indian brutality – above all the slaughtering of women and children – was compelling proof of inherent Indian viciousness. This viciousness was adduced to transform territorial aggression against Indians into defensive action, saving the lives of white women and children and preserving the civilization they embodied.[1] Thus, the Indian story depended for its morality on gender distinctions between its white characters, casting men as active defenders, women as passive representations of that which was defended.

In many of these Indian tales the possibility of marriage between a white woman and an Indian man – never the reverse – raised the question of whether white and Indian civilizations might be conjoined. The answer was always no. White women who were forced into such marriages were in no position to impose civilized values on their captors; the white woman who chose to marry an Indian had already rejected civilization and thus could not represent it. Either way, white women married to Indians did not civilize them but became Indianized themselves. The stories maintained, then, that in order to represent white civilization, white women had to remain within its protective and defining boundaries.

The many women writers of Indian tales agreed that Indian and white cultures were incompatible, and they accepted – indeed welcomed – their role as representatives of white civilization. They argued, however, that if white women did represent civilization, as men claimed, then they should be shown as having a greater role in it. Specifically, white women's capacity to sympathize with the unfortunate might have a pacifying effect on the vanquished Indians. Male writers countered by insisting that Indian-white violence was inevitable. The topic of whites and Indians across cultures merged with the topic of male and female within white culture.

The self-conscious merging of gender and Indian issues may be seen when we put *The Last of the Mohicans* in its historical network of men's and women's Indian stories that revised each other from gendered perspectives. Two Indian stories by men – the epic poem *Yamoyden* (1820) by James W. Eastburn and Robert C. Sands, and *The Pioneers* by James Fenimore Cooper (1823) – inspired Lydia Maria Child's *Hobomok* (1824); this novel in turn affected Cooper's next Indian book, *The Last of the Mohicans* (1826); and *The Last of the Mohicans* spurred Catharine Maria Sedgwick to write *Hope Leslie* (1827).

Lydia Maria Child was moved to write her first novel *Hobomok* when she read a long review of *Yamoyden* in an old copy of the prestigious New England journal, the *North American Review.*[2] Several of *Hobomok*'s chapter epigraphs are taken from *Yamoyden*, as is the skeleton of its plot. *Hobomok*'s framing preface refers to Cooper and specifically to *The Pioneers*, which is clearly the model for several of its scenes. Thus the work openly identifies itself with specific narrative precursors by men, affiliating with them yet inviting readers to notice deviations from them.

Yamoyden, a verse epic, is set during King Philip's War (1676–77) against the Puritans. One element of its variegated plot features Nora, a young Puritan woman who has married the "friendly" and Christianized Indian Yamoyden and has been disowned by her father as a result. In the tumult of interracial and intertribal war, Yamoyden is killed by an Indian bullet aimed at Nora's father, Nora dies of grief and exhaustion by his side, and the remorseful and belatedly forgiving father adopts their child. Though the poem was sympathetic to the Indian cause — so much so that the *North American*'s reviewer complained that its New York authors had "gone out of their way to throw a gauntlet to New England" — the Indians lose everything, and the white woman affiliated with an Indian (even an exemplary Christian one) dies.

Indian warfare in *The Pioneers*, which takes place in mid-state New York during 1793–94, is a thing of the past. Only one aged Indian — who will become the lordly Chingachgook in *The Last of the Mohicans* — remains in the area. Nevertheless, Indian wrongs are very much in the foreground, for the question of land ownership on which the story turns is developed in constant reference to the dispossessed Indians. An Indian-white marriage as a way to redress past wrongs seems possible, because the heiress-heroine has no suitor in the wilderness and there is a very handsome and exceptionally well-bred young man in the vicinity who would be ideal for her — except that he is thought to be a grandson of Chingachgook. This possible outcome is aborted, however, when he turns out to be the grandson of an American Tory; the marriage closes the gap that the Revolution had opened between England and the United States rather than the chasm between two groups of Americans competing for the same space.

Child sets her *Hobomok* in Salem, Massachusetts, between 1629 and 1633, so early in the history of New England settlement that no major war between Indians and whites had yet been fought. The Conant family at the novel's center contains a tyrannical, middle-class Puritan father and his aristocratic Anglican wife and daughter whom he has transported from their comfortable life in England to the American wilderness. Mrs. Conant soon sickens and dies from overwork in the New World. The daughter, Mary, deprived of her mother, her friends (one dies, another moves away), and her Anglican lover (who is banished from the house by her father and then presumed lost at sea), becomes distraught. Her father's unrelenting harshness, his immersion in abstract doctrinal controversy, and his lack of sympathy for his daughter drive her into the arms of the friendly Indian Hobomok, who has long worshipped her from afar. After three years of marriage Mary returns to the Puritan community without stigma and with her son, to marry her first love (he was not dead after all). Mary's contrite father changes from severe Puritan into doting grandfather, and Mary's son forgets his Indian beginnings.

How could this finale come about? Mary is able to rejoin white society and marry Charles Brown, her early love, because when he returns, Hobomok officially divorces her, Indian-style, and then chooses to "vanish" into the forest. Hobomok does these things because he knows that all these years Mary has continued to love Charles – he does it for *her*. As for *Indian* women – Hobomok has made enemies of other Indians, and in particular of the malignant Corbitant (who stalks around the margins of the novel threatening but never achieving violence), because he declined to marry Corbitant's sister. He rejected Indian women because he perceived intuitively that Mary was superior to all of them. The narrator offers Hobomok's sense of Mary's superiority as proof of *Hobomok's* superiority. Hobomok is different from other Indians, better than other Indians, because he takes Mary seriously as embodying a better civilization than his own. And if an untutored Indian can take Mary seriously, then surely (it is implied) the advanced men of her own culture ought to do so also.

If Hobomok's marriage ennobles him, Mary's does not ennoble her. It does not lower her either, but only because it is an aberration, attributable to the mental depression for which her father was really to blame. Kinder paternal treatment would have prevented this calamity, as the father comes to realize and to rue. Hobomok, then, is mostly a pawn in Mary's eventually successful power struggle with her father. Her enduring second marriage (her real marriage, we might say) to a Church of England man recapitulates Cooper's decision in *The Pioneers* to unite Old and New England rather than Indian and white.

These events allow Mary to escape the destiny her father had in mind for her and give her a value independent of men's plans. More generally, *Hobomok* gives to women, at least to some women, the power to reform white society by bringing about change in men, as Mary brings about change in her father. The novel implies that to implement women's values and woman-centered values would be to create a less intolerant, less literal-minded, more gracious civil state than the one instituted in America by Puritan men. The novel implies that such a civil state has already been created in New England, for it is a *historical* novel about things that have already happened, and its story is basically about how a woman has softened the Puritan male heart and thereby created a better society for all. For all, that is, except Indians.

Thus, we might see *Hobomok* as finally less about Indians versus whites than about white women versus white men, and especially about white women's desire to be recognized and empowered within male-dominated white society. From this perspective, the novel would seem to pose little threat to the male version of Indian-white relations. Nevertheless the very fact that the book was organized as a female-centered narrative about the progress of civilization could be perceived as a challenge to white male ownership of the Indian-white narrative, which is to say white male ownership of history itself.

Two women speak plainly in this novel, the author and her heroine. No matter *why* Mary gave herself to Hobomok, she did it; and the sexuality of the union produces a child whose presence cannot be ignored. The novel also shows Mary's increasing affection for Hobomok over time. With his good looks, his high ideals, his romantic love for Mary, his excellence as husband and father, Hobomok is a perfect fantasy lover – at once romantic, sexual, and domestic – who puts in question the adequacies and pretensions of white men. From a white male perspective, Hobomok might seem too attractive a representation of an Indian male for an audience containing many women.

In addition, the ease with which Mary transfers her affections from Charles Brown to Hobomok and back again implies a certain erotic plasticity that did not comport with the white woman's role as a stable and self-negating icon of civilization. The fact that one of Mary's spouses is a "native" and the other a high-class Church of England man makes the Puritan males' world view look somewhat parochial. Child's suggestion that American Puritan women were more aristocratic than their men hints that the Puritans' religious creed might embody class origins rather than the divine word.[3] Associating Puritan women with both Indians and Old

71

World aristocracy, Child's fable could make the ongoing male project of subduing the American continent appear vulnerable to inter-
nal sabotage from a range of intellectual positions.

Cooper was no admirer of the New England patriarchy, but he
seems to have taken *Hobomok* as a challenge to his own views. *The
Last of the Mohicans* may be seen as an attempt to disparage Child's
novel as a juvenile and potentially harmful fantasy. *The Last of the
Mohicans* insists that white men's repressive representations of the
feminine are valid, and uses the romanticizing of Indians in wom-
en's novels as evidence of the unfitness of women for the cultural
responsibility to which they aspired. Cooper's many-stranded argument depends on the fundamental claim that his novels represent Indian warfare and Indian nature realistically, whereas wom-
en's novels represent nothing but feminine ignorance. The gender
distinction is not an accident. Men could produce realism because
they faced reality directly; women could produce only schoolgirl
romance because they were protected – by men – from the
ceaseless struggle through which civilization is instituted and
maintained, as well as from the savagery that makes the struggle
necessary. Ironically but crucially, the protected space that women
would reject in order to play a more active part in the world is
exactly what has enabled them to imagine the utopian alternative
they mistake for truth. Only men can write truthfully – only men
can write truthfully even about women.

Compared to *The Pioneers, The Last of the Mohicans* is much more
concerned with the place of women characters in a social polity,
and it makes explicit the implicit question of sex between Indian
men and white women. The novel uses Cora and Alice to consider
alternative ways of writing women into the story of white colonization of the North American continent. This opposition is developed in a context where any possible connection between a
sympathetic white woman and a friendly noble Indian is nullified
in advance by the reality of hatred and difference between the
races. In his dichotomy of Cora and Alice, Cooper asks how an
embattled civilization might use such active traits as outspoken
bravery, firmness, intelligence, self-possession, and eloquence in a
woman. By developing these attributes in a woman whom the
novel discards for one who has been socially constructed as an

object, he makes his answer clear: In a woman, these traits are of no use at all. Although Alice's extreme passivity constantly endangers her and her companions, it turns out that it is precisely in preserving this woman that a civilization signifies itself. In *The Last of the Mohicans,* a white man does not need a woman fighting by his side to inspire him, still less a woman mediating between him and the Indian enemy; he needs a woman to fight *for* and to fight *about*. White women best serve the white nation by sacrificing their dangerous dreams of independent selfhood, reining in their wandering sexual fantasies, and recognizing that they are most useful to civilization as protected possessions of white men.

The Last of the Mohicans obviously rejects the woman-centered structure of *Hobomok,* reclaiming the Indian story for white men. The novel's center is occupied by Duncan Heyward, a very white white man. Cooper's procedure in this (as in his other books) is to represent almost everything from the outside, through a narrator voice that records the externally visible details of action without much explanation, seldom venturing into any character's mind. The only mind entered regularly is Duncan Heyward's. We often read of his feelings, his attention, his painful doubt, his hope, his confidence, his hearing, his fancies, his shame, his uneasiness, his interest, his belief (pp. 81, 129, 191, 204). The only other mind entered (and much less often) is Cora's.

Moreover, Duncan's line of sight organizes the action, and some awkward plotting (like his ludicrous disguise to enter the Huron camp) is required to carry this through consistently. Duncan is present in every scene in the book, and all of them are viewed from his perspective except for the Fort William Henry Massacre. He functions in the novel as the reader's surrogate, the position from which readers would view the action if they were *in* the action, and he is the patriarch's lieutenant and his heir, that is, the present and future protector of the American woman and through her, protector and progenitor of American civilization. The plot seems to be about rescuing two women from Indians; in actuality, it rescues one woman – Duncan's woman. At the same time it eliminates the alternative couple, Uncas and Cora, and thus decrees that the future nation will be peopled by whites only.

Because she is unsuitable for Duncan Cora is fatally paired with

Uncas; one needs to ask why she is ineligible to marry the novel's technical hero. It is sometimes maintained that Cora holds no interest for Duncan but is of great interest to both Magua and Uncas because of her trace of black blood. No doubt discovery of her "taint" affects Duncan, a southerner, adversely. He was already in love with Alice, however, before Major Munro explained the different origins of his two daughters, and neither Uncas nor Magua ever knows anything of the matter. Moreover – and this is important – Magua dismisses blacks as a lower order of being in a speech that articulates the metaphysics of his tribe:

> "The spirit that made men, coloured them differently," commenced the subtle Huron. "Some are blacker than the sluggish bear. These he said should be slaves; and he ordered them to work for ever, like the beaver. You may hear them groan, when the south wind blows, louder than the lowing buffaloes, along the shores of the great salt lake, where the big canoes come and go with them in droves." (pp. 300–1)

Critics following the examples of D. H. Lawrence and Leslie Fiedler suggest that Cora's blackness symbolizes her unacceptable sexuality, her covert affinity for Indians. The "impurity" in her blood is taken to stand for what Cooper would have wanted his audience to accept as a *moral* impurity. Cooper works hard in the narrative, however, to prevent readers from reaching this conclusion, stridently asserting Cora's moral purity on every possible occasion. Moreover the story he wants to tell would be meaningless if Cora were morally flawed. Certainly, she is attractive *to* Indians as Alice is not. She is the object of a lustful appraisal from Magua that Alice could never inspire: "Her eyes sunk with shame under an impression, that, for the first time, they had encountered an expression that no chaste female might endure" (p. 105).

Not Cora, but Magua and the typical Indian view of women that he exemplifies, are the narrator's probable targets here. Part of the way in which Magua has earlier been unfavorably characterized involves his scorn for the respectful protection with which white men treat white women: "The pale-faces make themselves dogs to their women . . . and when they want to eat, their warriors must lay aside the tomahawk to feed their laziness" (p. 42). These words bode ill for any white woman who might become his victim. It is a low opinion of women rather than some unrepressed primitive appreciation of their sexuality that Magua shows the reader in his open display of lust for Cora.

If Cora's blackness does not imply suppressed sexual desire or moral impurity, what might it be doing in this story? As the adored, even favorite, daughter of a father who married women of two different races (although Cora's mother was only remotely descended from black slaves), she could function as the possible progenitor of an American future in which the races were combined. Her already mixed blood, mixed again with an Indian's, would produce triracial children – the incarnate "e pluribus unum" of the American national seal. This suggestive function for Cora coincides with the novelistic convention that requires youthful characters to be romantically paired. Given Duncan's clear preference for Alice, the plot *must* continually invite readers to look for a man for Cora. Cora's mixed blood and lack of race prejudice (she alone among the white characters refuses to judge Indians on the basis of skin color) make it theoretically possible for her to marry an Indian, especially since Duncan is the only romantically eligible white male in the novel.

The novel thus has two simultaneously developed plots. One is Duncan's quest to rescue Alice; the other is a struggle over Cora between *two* Indians, both of whom desire her, one instrumentally (like a savage), and one idealistically (like a civilized man). An obvious outcome toward which this second plot might be tending is that Cora will marry Uncas after he has killed Magua. Everything in the second half of the book – everything following the massacre at Fort William Henry in Chapter 17 – encourages a reader to expect this possibility. Uncas demonstrates his devotion to Cora in the zeal with which he finds and keeps a trail invisible to everybody else; his astonishing bravery and fortitude are made clear in the captivity scenes; and when he appears at the Delaware village he is installed as the great chief of a resurgent Indian nation that could, perhaps, flourish and coexist with whites on the North American continent. "Bad" whites (French) and "bad" Indians (Hurons) would be eliminated, and "good" representatives of the two races, English whites and Delaware Indians, would become one family through marriage to sisters.

That, Cooper says sternly, is fantasy. We know what really happened, we know how history turned out.

Let us now retrace our steps somewhat, and ask: If it is not some subliminal response to the sexuality of her black blood that makes Cora attractive to Indians and not to Duncan, then what is it? Consider Duncan's farewell (Chapter 15) to the two sisters. "'God bless you in every fortune, noble – Cora – I may, and must call you. . . . In every fortune, I know you will be an ornament and honour to your sex. Alice, adieu' – his tone changed from admiration to tenderness – 'adieu, Alice; we shall soon meet again'" (p. 150). To admire is to think highly of, which implies that the person so thought of is above the person doing the thinking, and hence in no need of any help from that person. Tenderness is the solicitude and concern called out in a stronger person by the appeal of one who is weaker; it is a response to the expression of need. Unlike admiration, tenderness involves – perhaps requires – some kind of possessiveness. The relationship of "love" in which white men and women are paired asymmetrically involves the male response of protective tenderness toward the woman's display of dependent weakness.

It is evident that Alice fulfills the implicit definition here of a lovable woman. She is artless, thoughtless, childlike, cheerful, and consistently unable to fend for herself. She clings to Duncan "with the dependency of an infant" and is drawn into the cavern by Cora in a "nearly insensible" state (p. 80), a "trembling weeper" on her firmer sister's maternal bosom (p. 82). She regards Duncan with a look of "infantile dependency" (p. 108). She looks "like some beautiful emblem of the wounded delicacy of her sex, devoid of animation, and yet keenly conscious" (p. 110). During the retreat from Fort William Henry, she drops "senseless on the earth" and her dead faint enables Magua to abduct her and thus lure Cora to eventual doom (pp. 177–8). When Duncan finds Alice in captivity, she is trembling "in a manner which betrayed her inability to stand"; "helpless" to follow him, she has to be carried out of the cave, a "precious burthen," later a "precious and nearly insensible burthen" (pp. 259, 262, 263, 264, 303).

Yet Alice survives whereas her sister, the noble-minded maiden, the paragon of fortitude, ends up a "burthen" carried to her grave by a bevy of Delaware women. Thus, it would seem, Alice's very tenderness and softness, her constant need to be tended, watched over, taken care of, finally save her, but Cora's very strength, her firmness, boldness, fortitude, and thoughtfulness have the opposite result. A woman's weakness *is* her strength in the white world, because it inspires men like Duncan, representative of European-American civilization, to fight for her. Cora endorses this idea, as we see in her assumption of a protective, maternal role toward her sister throughout the novel.[4] In her parting words to Duncan when she leaves as Magua's captive — "I need not tell you to cherish the treasure you will possess" (p. 316) — Cora describes Alice as a "treasure" who can be possessed.

Alice's fitness to be loved by men of white culture does not translate to anything that an Indian, even a "good" Indian, can understand. She is of no interest to Magua *or* to Uncas. Alice would be a burden, but no treasure, to an Indian male. The gendered interrelation of dependency and protection — "love" — does not exist among Indians. This does not mean, however, that women and men are more nearly equal in Indian culture. Magua, seeking revenge against Munro by treating his daughter like an Indian, rejects Alice as unsuitable for his design, but he certainly does not appreciate Cora for the qualities that make her admirable to the representative white male Duncan Heyward. Magua appreciates Cora's strength and fortitude because they mean she will be good for drawing water, hoeing corn, cooking venison, and binding up his battle wounds (p. 105). According to white standards, his is a double devaluing of women: First, he sees Cora as an object in a hostile exchange between two men (Magua and Munro), and second, he sees her as a possession to be used, to be used up, in attending to his physical demands. Women in Indian societies are no less possessions, but much more beasts of burden, slaves, than in white. As was typical in his day among whites who studied Indian culture, Cooper argues that the Indian shows himself to be a savage above all in his uncivilized treatment of women.

In making this argument, Cooper endorses the white woman's interest in love and in love stories. *The Last of the Mohicans* maintains that love in the Western sense is very much in a woman's interest and insists that such love is only encountered in the civilization that has invented it. The novel rejects women's fantasies of Indian lovers from the perspective of a historical understanding that love is a white cultural construction, existing only in white society.[5]

It could be objected to this line of interpretation that Magua, in his attitudes toward women is only one individual, not a generic Indian. But Cooper's development of the Indian presence in *The Last of the Mohicans* makes Magua (rather than Uncas) the epitome of Indian society. His name is a simple variation of his tribe's name – Maqua – which identifies the whole Iroquois confederacy. Magua's oratorical success with his people comes from his ability to articulate their beliefs. Cooper observes that authority among Indians is a very perilous and provisional matter, because Indians are so fiercely democratic – all the more reason to conclude that Magua has power *over* them exactly and only insofar as he stands *for* them (p. 92). Although Magua is heroized as a Miltonian Prince of Darkness, the Indians are also represented as diabolic and demoniac figures, emerging from the gloom of the forest with satanic yells, possessed of a virtually supernatural ability to materialize and dematerialize. This reflects a tradition that goes back to Puritan allegories in the earliest captivity narratives, where Indians were seen, literally, as fiends.

On a more mundane note, we observe that Cora's plea to be rescued by Tamenund, the sage of the alternative Delaware tribe, is rejected in terms showing that where women are concerned, there is little difference between opposing Indian cultures: "Girl, what wouldst thou! A great warrior takes thee to wife. Go – thy race will not end" (p. 313). If we turn to Uncas as an alternative representation of the Indian, we discover that Uncas's sympathetic and sentimental side (that enables him to love and admire Cora for herself) "elevated him far above the intelligence, and advanced him probably centuries before the practices of his nation" (p. 115). Thus, Uncas is a fit partner for Cora not because he is like an Indian, but because in crucial ways he is unlike an Indian.

Cora leaves the Delaware camp as Magua's "passive captive" (p. 317). The words alert us to the reality in *The Last of the Mohicans* that Cora's firmness and boldness and fortitude, even though they

78

distinguish her from her weaker sister, finally mean nothing in this novel's larger world. As Magua's captive, Cora is as much an object as Alice. Hawk-eye refers to both women equally as "harmless things," "flowers," "tender blossoms," "gentle ones" (pp. 46, 127, 138); the narrator speaks of both women's "fragile forms" (pp. 93, 261). To both, the women are interchangeable. In the warrior world of *The Last of the Mohicans*, no degree of difference between Cora and Alice will finally make Cora into a man who can fight and kill. Since she is not a man, she can only be a woman. When Magua proposes to exchange Cora for Hawk-eye, the scout replies, "It would be an unequal exchange, to give a warrior, in the prime of his age and usefulness, for the best woman on the frontiers" (p. 314). The inferior physical strength of a woman makes anatomy her destiny, because in war the issue is quickly and finally one of brute force.

If the Indians had possessed even some of the whites' reverence for womanhood, the story implies, the novel's final catastrophe would not have happened nor would the massacre at Fort William Henry have occurred. The massacre, which the denouement in a sense repeats, is the novel's rhetorical and thematic centerpiece. Among a variety of possible incidents in the sources he drew on for his account, Cooper selected a scene of wanton woman-killing to epitomize the whole. Indians greedy for finery, overcome by blood lust, and desperate for scalps to demonstrate their manhood make no distinction among victims; the helplessness of the women makes it easier for them to achieve their goals. The scene presumably has particular horror for white readers, but this is because they *do* make the distinction.

Cooper thus places the story of his two women in a world at war, a world in which women are better served by warriors who give special status to women than by warriors who do not. The plot of *The Last of the Mohicans* is a concrete instance of the novel's world, an example of the fate of women in a world whose norm is war. Everything that happens within the plot's enclosure resonates with the combat that surrounds and occasions it. The action unfolds as a repetitious series of retreats from one space of supposed safety to another, each refuge quickly turning into a space of ferocious combat. The battle for possession of the entire continent makes the entire continent a scene of bloodshed, with no certain safety anywhere.

The general combat is not restricted to Indian versus white; the French and Indian wars are represented as a territorial struggle between whites, with traditionally hostile Indian tribes enlisted on competing sides. Moreover, the French, victorious at Fort William Henry, are shown as permitting the Indians' massacre to take place. Because war-making in *The Last of the Mohicans* is an activity engaged in by all men, the novel does not especially blame the Indians. War is inevitable when different cultural groups aspire to the same territory; the particular history narrated in the novel began when whites invaded the American continent, when the French and English "united to rob the untutored possessors of its wooded scenery of their native right" to the land (p. 12), and the Dutch deployed liquor to cheat the Indians of both land and dignity. Magua is the novel's chief victim as well as its chief villain. "Is it justice to make evil, and then punish for it!" he exclaims rhetorically to Cora, and she, like other white characters in Indian stories confronted by arguments they cannot counter, must simply remain silent, thereby acknowledging that the Indians are right (p. 103).

Cora's silence implies more than the justness of the Indian cause; it also means that justice is irrelevant to the reality the novel urges on its readers. Dreams of domesticated Indians and peacefully cohabiting settlements are constituents of a girlish imagination, an imagination perhaps typical in a young woman like Alice, who is pleased to sing hymns too loudly with David Gamut in the wilderness. This imagination, though charming and an appropriate expression of female inexperience, is not harmless, however, because its illusion of safety creates vulnerability, just as the noisy harmony alerts hostile Indians to the whereabouts of the white party. The fancy that Indians like Hobomok will nobly vanish into the forest after they have been badly cheated and treated – will do so out of love and admiration for what a white woman represents – is even sillier, from Cooper's perspective. The kind of woman that civilization has created and protects is useful only when she *is* protected; should a woman like this attempt to act on the basis of what she believes about the world, the result could only be disaster. The counterattempt to undermine the fantasies on the basis of which civilized (hence unworldly) women might be tempted to intervene in the world, may be part of the strategy of the repeated scenes of breached security in *The Last of the Mohicans*.

The assumption that men's depictions of a warrior world are realistic for all times and places whereas women's more pacific representations are always and everywhere dangerously utopian, institutes gender distinction at the most fundamental narrative level. This claim to superior realism on the grounds of greater worldliness characterizes much of men's writing throughout American history, from Cooper to Ernest Hemingway and beyond. That Cooper had women's narratives in mind when writing *The Last of the Mohicans* is bluntly asserted in his preface to the first edition of the book, which announces that the story relates "to matters which may not be universally understood, especially by the more imaginative sex, some of whom, under the impression that it is a fiction, may be induced to read the book," and which inveighs against readers "who find a strange gratification in spending more of their time in making books, than of their money in buying them" (p. 1). It concludes by advising "all young ladies, whose ideas are usually limited by the four walls of a comfortable drawing room," to avoid *The Last of the Mohicans* since "after they have read the book, they will surely pronounce it shocking" (p. 4).

Maria Sedgwick's *Hope Leslie* appeared a year after *The Last of the Mohicans*. It might have been subtitled *The Last of the Pequods,* so closely did it invoke its precursor while at the same time spiritedly challenging it. The challenge begins with the preface, which cheerfully grants that this novel, like all novels, is not history but fiction and implicitly mocks Cooper's insistence that his own story is anything else. Throughout the novel, Sedgwick counters Cooper's male severity and rigidity with a feminine sprightliness. Hope Leslie, her heroine, is a young woman with a decided taste for fun and laughter. More somberly, Sedgwick denies that any account of Indians and whites told from an exclusive white viewpoint can be true; by promising an Indian perspective she in effect offers her own account as more historical than Cooper's. This beginning is followed by the surprising representation of the Uncas figure as an

Indian woman, a depiction that cannot but bring strongly to the reader's mind the functional absence of Indian women from Cooper's narrative. And the novel quickly develops the likelihood of two Indian-white marriages, one of which takes place.

Hope Leslie opens in New England immediately after the first Pequod war of the late 1630s. Its first half takes place on the frontier, and features Indian massacres, daring rescues, and escapes. It looks like a typical Indian story except for its audacious sex-role reversal, with the young hero Everell Fletcher (the Duncan Heyward figure) saved by the sacrifice of the young Indian woman Magawisca, daughter of the defeated Pequod chief. Magawisca recalls Pocahontas; her initial conflict between love for Everell (and his family, in which she has been indentured since her capture), and love for her father suggests a possible outcome like the marriage between Pocahontas and John Rolfe. In rescuing her, however, her father massacres most of the Fletcher household, and New England history takes a different turn from Virginia history. Enabling Everell to escape from her father (a deed that involves the loss of her arm as she wards off a blow aimed for Everell), Magawisca gives him up to white culture and to the white heroine, Hope Leslie.

Sedgwick gleefully announces that she will refrain from describing, "step by step, the progress of the Indian fugitives," since their "sagacity in traversing their native forests" has been "so well described in a recent popular work, that their usages have become familiar as household words, and nothing remains but to shelter defects of skill and knowledge under the veil of silence."[6] After this pointed allusion to *The Last of the Mohicans* she goes on to do what, presumably, she does have the skill and knowledge to do (perhaps what Cooper cannot do?) – describe civilized society. The second part of the novel is set in Boston several years later and in many respects reads like a different work; it largely combines a drawing-room comedy of romantic misunderstanding with a gothic melodrama featuring a villainous Catholic disguised as a Puritan with evil designs on the heroine. This heroine, Hope Leslie, replaces Magawisca as the focus of reader interest and of Everell's affections.

Magawisca's reappearance, however, returns the fiction to the Indian/woman connection because she brings Hope news of her sister Faith, who has married Magawisca's brother Oneco. In the intervening years Magawisca has become irremediably Indian, so there is no longer any question of marriage between her and Everell. Faith is similarly lost to white society, having become wholly Indianized by her marriage. She is different from Magawisca, however, to whom she is contrasted much as Alice is contrasted to Cora – one is intractably independent, the other completely dependent on her male protector and provider. Faith's dependency makes her impervious to white culture's attempts to reclaim her; she wants only to be with Oneco.

In another ingenious reversal of Cooper, the novel features the capture and rescue of these two *Indian* women. Faith is kidnapped by the Puritan establishment and incarcerated in Governor Winthrop's mansion to be rehabilitated; eventually Oneco arrives in disguise (just as Duncan disguised himself to get to Alice) and carries her off. Magawisca is unjustly accused of fomenting Indian hostility against the Puritans and is imprisoned. In a scene recalling the escape of Natty Bumppo from prison in *The Pioneers,* Hope and Everell release her – but this event follows a trial scene during which Magawisca voices the uncompromising alienation of Indian from white culture: "Take my own word, I am your enemy; the sun-beam and the shadow cannot mingle. The white man cometh – the Indian vanisheth. Can we grasp in friendship the hand raised to strike us?"[7]

When Hope and Everell plead with her to "return and dwell with us," she replies: "My own people have been spoiled – we cannot take as a gift that which is our own – the law of vengeance is written on our hearts – you say you have a written rule of forgiveness – it may be better – if ye would be guided by it – it is not for us – the Indian and the white man can no more mingle, and become one, than day and night."[8] She thus simultaneously criticizes white people for failure to act on their own law of forgiveness, and exempts the Indians from the need to act on a law not their own. Magawisca might have defended herself by pointing out that she was not guilty as charged; she chooses rather to claim that she did not owe obedience to laws of another nation than her own. This defense undermines the possibility of societal pluralism.

Just as Magawisca repels white advances toward her, so Faith Leslie rejects the white world in her marriage. "No speak Yengeese" are her first – and virtually the only – words she speaks to Hope, and her "final departure" does not "seriously disturb" Hope's happiness. "There had been nothing in the intercourse of the sisters to excite Hope's affections. Faith had been spiritless, woe-begone – a soulless body – and had repelled, with sullen indifference, all Hope's efforts to win her love."[9] *Hope Leslie* presents Indians as inaccessible to all white attempts to acculturate them and offers no social alternative to acculturation. Hence the novel, despite its representations of a noble woman savage and a white woman married to an Indian, serves a purpose much like Cooper's after all. Sedgwick's three surviving Pequods and Faith voluntarily "vanish" into the western forests. Out of sight, out of the white mind from whose transgendered perspective the novel proceeds, they are never heard from again.

In its second part *Hope Leslie*, like *Hobomok*, focuses on an intra-cultural transaction between white man and white women more than on an extracultural story of whites and Indians. It also tells the same intracultural story that *Hobomok* did of the moderating of Puritan severity under feminine influence. Hope, abetted by Ever-ell, has engineered Magawisca's escape from jail; she should be severely punished, but Governor Winthrop declines to act harshly. His mildness, evoked by a woman's spirited heterodoxy, justifies the New England errand into the wilderness, demonstrating that the Puritans were capable of rising above their initial narrow-minded bigotry. It does not matter to this interpretation that the New England settlement meant the displacement of Indians, be-cause the Indians chose to go.

Indian stories were published in quantity into the 1830s (after a hiatus they reappeared as "westerns," a new form recognizing that most of the Indians remaining on the continent had been settled west of the Mississippi). In Cooper's 1827 *The Prairie*, the passive woman is a much more grotesque figure than Alice and the active woman is a much more healthy, ordinary person than Cora. In his

1829 novel, *The Wept of Wish-ton-Wish*, Cooper ventured into the specific domain of the New England Indian story, portraying a white-Indian marriage resembling the marriage of Faith and Oneco with disastrous consequences for the white woman and her family of origin.

Even more striking traces of women's Indian stories in his work can be seen in the later additions to the Leatherstocking saga. *The Pathfinder* (1840) and *The Deerslayer* (1841) both give white women far more centrality than did the three early books, allow them much more active roles, and create important Indian women characters. Although never granting any woman full partnership with men in the defense of culture, Cooper apparently came to see that no radical overthrow of patriarchy followed when women became more equally involved in the action. He perhaps also recognized that women readers, comprising the main audience for fiction, had to be satisfied if he was to make a living as an author.

His works never abandoned, however, a representation of a world in which everybody had membership in a cultural group and in which each group was always in violent and unforgiving competition with other cultural groups for possession of scarce goods. Curiously, it may have been the defiant Magawisca and the retrograde Faith Leslie who showed Cooper how to bring such entities as martial white women, Indian-white marriage, and Indian women within the scope of this world view.

NOTES

1. For the historical context in which Indian stories developed, see Roy Harvey Pearce, *The Savages of America: A Study of the Indian and the Idea of Civilization* (Baltimore: Johns Hopkins, rev. ed. 1965); Bernard W. Sheehan, *Seeds of Extinction: Jeffersonian Philanthropy and the American Indian* (Chapel Hill: University of North Carolina Press, 1973); Richard Slotkin, *Regeneration Through Violence: The Mythology of the American Frontier, 1600–1860* (Middletown, Conn.: Wesleyan University Press, 1973); Francis Jennings, *The Invasion of America: Indians, Colonialism, and the Cant of Conquest* (Chapel Hill: University of North Carolina Press, 1975); Michael Paul Rogin, *Fathers and Children: Andrew Jackson and the Subjugation of the American Indian* (New York: Alfred A. Knopf,

1975); and Richard Drinnon, *Facing West: The Metaphysics of Indian-Hating and Empire-Building* (New York: New American Library, 1980). For an argument that the approach of women writers to frontier experience was different from men's, see Annette Kolodny, *The Land Before Her: Fantasy and Experience of the American Frontiers, 1630–1860* (Chapel Hill: University of North Carolina Press, 1984).

2. *Hobomok and Other Writings on Indians by Lydia Maria Child,* ed. Carolyn Karcher (New Brunswick: Rutgers University Press, 1986), p. xviii.

3. *Hobomok* is richly detailed in its descriptions of doctrinal controversy; although this dimension of the novel cannot be developed here, its degree of expertise and involvement in these matters emphasizes the point that Child's main interest is intracultural.

4. Cora's maternal behavior invites a psychological or anthropological reading of Duncan's resistance to her, as though she were a "mother" and therefore taboo to the son, or as though she were a sexually experienced woman and therefore already owned by some other man. In both readings, however, society would be composed of men who *own* property and women who *are* property.

5. A common version of today's popular female romance is the self-styled "Indian romance" pairing an Indian man with a white woman and ending when the woman abandons white civilization for her Indian lover. Examples can be found at the supermarket checkout line. Some of the many titles in the subgenre (all 1989 copyrights) are *Renegade Heart* (Apache), *Night Flame* (Cheyenne), and *Savage Heat* (Sioux).

6. Maria Sedgwick, *Hope Leslie; or, Early Times in Massachusetts,* ed. Mary Kelley (New Brunswick: Rutgers University Press, 1987), p. 81.

7. Ibid., p. 292.

8. Ibid., p. 330.

9. Ibid., p. 338.

5

Generation through Violence: Cooper and the Making of Americans

SHIRLEY SAMUELS

A N early analogue to the slaughter of women and children in *The Last of the Mohicans* is the surprising sacrifice of the colt, who "gliding like a fallow deer" follows its mother into the forest (p. 22). The colt's resemblance to a deer turns out to be ominous: The first deer that appears in the novel has a knife passed "across the throat," after which it is proposed to "cut our steaks, and let the carcass drive down the stream" (pp. 35, 51). When Natty Bumppo decrees, "That colt, at least, must die," Chingachgook's "knife passed across its throat quicker than thought, and . . . he dashed it into the river, down whose stream it glided away" (p. 47). Such killings in Cooper, acts of violence "quicker than thought," have traditionally been seen in mythic and sacrificial terms.[1] This way of reading emphasizes the ritualistic character of these frontier rites of passage, mythologizing the act of entering the wilderness, but it also, perhaps inevitably, ignores the specific transformations of identity involved in such violence. In *The Last of the Mohicans,* these killings conflate domestic and wild, suggesting the conflation of animals and humans throughout the novel; beyond that, the explanations given for them point to the renegotiation of the racial and sexual identities of Indian and white, male and female.

Responding to the threat to his colt, David Gamut confers on it almost human status: "spare the foal of Miriam! It is the comely offspring of a faithful dam" (p. 47). Natty Bumppo accuses him of betraying his species: "it wont be long afore he submits to the rationality of killing a four-footed beast, to save the lives of human men" (p. 51). The "rationality" of killing the colt to save the lives of "human men," however, does not seem as significant as the

87

attempt to specify discriminations that the novel repeatedly transgresses and reasserts, transgressions and reassertions that in their very restlessness raise the question of what recognition is being enforced, or what difference is being asserted between, it would seem, nonhuman and human men, or human men and women. The animal's death appears logically unnecessary, but thematically significant in initiating a series of lessons in categorical distinctions – "human men," "four-footed beast" – in which physical embodiments become emblematic and the emblematic gets embodied.

Natty Bumppo first contrasts and then conflates the value of life for animals and the value of life for humans; he notes both the difference between beasts and men and the danger of losing "moments that are as precious as the heart's blood to a stricken deer" (p. 46), and in doing so he makes unsteady declarations of species. Whereas on the one hand he calls for the sacrifice of the colt for the survival of humans, on the other he equates the "heart's blood" of the deer with the precious moments of the hunter. Arguing further about the need to kill the colt, he asserts, "When men struggle for the single life God has given them . . . even their own kind seem no more than the beasts of the wood" (p. 47). This analogy may be designed to justify the (forthcoming) killing of humans as though they were animals, but its implicit contradiction emphasizes how much the struggle in the woods becomes a struggle to stabilize identities rather than to respect already stable distinctions of "kind."[2] These instabilities are registered, for instance, in the name given to Uncas, "le cerf agile" or "the nimble deer" (p. 91), a name ironically juxtaposed to one of Natty's alternative identities as the deerslayer or, again, to the name he calls his rifle, "kill-deer." Alternately personifying and dehumanizing, these names point to the violent struggle in the novel to locate personhood.

Hence if there appears to be something gratuitous about killing "Miriam's foal," then to motivate such a gratuitous act entails comparisons that call attention to the formation of a peculiarly elusive species identity. If killing the foal appears neither necessary for the characters' escape nor sufficiently motivated as a mythic sacrifice to enter the wilderness, it seems rather to force the fundamental question of how the crossings of animals, humans, and landscapes produce identity. Leslie Fiedler has perceptively identified miscegenation as the "secret theme" of the Leatherstocking series.[3] In *The Last of the Mohicans*, frontier transactions involving animals and humans produce a radically crossed or miscegenated identity, producing, in effect, a miscegenation between nature and culture.[4]

One of the Indian legends Cooper may be drawing on, the Lenni-Lenape myth about the origin of human beings, their emergence from a dark and precultural underworld, involves a hunter encountering and killing a deer. Emerging from the underworld to the earth's surface, the hunter chases the deer into the wilderness and returns to his people with the meat. They then follow the hunter out into the world.[5] In this Indian legend, the drawing of human beings into culture is accomplished by the pursuit and consumption of the natural. The killing and eating of the animal explicitly leads the hunter to a sort of nature worship, a worship of a personified Mother Earth. The emergence of persons is thus linked to the marking of the difference between what's natural and what's cultural: nature worship only becomes possible once the separation between persons and nature has been violently effected.

What occupies the position of the natural and what occupies the position of the cultural in this narrative are violently shifted, however, by Cooper's anthropology. Rewriting the Indian legend, he substitutes the Indian for the deer followed into the forest, and traces a rather different genealogy of the origin of human civilization. It has been argued that the elegiac heroicizing of "the Indian" as natural man is only possible once his disappearance has been assured (the *last* of the Mohicans), but in Cooper this means a violent enacting of the difference between human men and what appear as nonhuman men.

Translating the tense negotiations about persons and places into the "hard facts" of Indian removal and massacre, Philip Fisher's account of Cooper tends to ratify such an elegiac inevitability of "the last" of the Mohicans.[6] In contrast, Richard Slotkin has suggested, about Cooper's Leatherstocking novels, that "as we cross the border between civilization and wilderness the 'normal' order of sexual and social values begins to be inverted."[7] I would argue instead that it is the location of these borders that is in question, or rather that setting and demarcating such borders is just what these crossings aim to accomplish. Such crossings affect not only how landscapes are figured but also how the making of persons gets figured, and it is the violent relation between the national landscape and the making of persons that I want to look at next.

The first person to become visible in the novel, David Gamut, displays a body and an identity that seem barely held together:

> He had all the bones and joints of other men, without any of their proportions. . . . His head was large; his shoulders narrow; his arms long and dangling; while his hands were small, if not delicate. His legs and thighs were thin nearly to emaciation, but of extraordinary length; and his knees would have been considered tremendous, had they not been outdone by the broader foundations on which this false superstructure of blended human orders, was so profanely reared. (p. 16)[8]

Gamut's lack of proportion is traced to a "false" and profane mixture of "blended human orders," a miscegenation that seems to place him in opposition to the often advertised "unmixed" blood of Chingachgook or Natty Bumppo, the "man without a cross." But also and more basically, the strange relations of his large head, narrow shoulders, and tremendous knees, the apparently borrowed "bones and joints of other men," show up here as a problem about how to put the body together; the architectural language of "superstructure" or "reared" suggests that the novel is returning to a primal scene of the emergence of persons or the taking apart of persons.

Gamut's opening remarks on Duncan Heyward's horse similarly treat the production and genealogy of bodies. The first character to speak in the novel, Gamut sings "forth the language of the holy book" to celebrate a "beast," which he loudly declares to be "not of home raising." He claims that the "barter and traffic in four-footed animals" would not include this animal, who seems to have "descended to our own time" "from the stock of the horse of Israel" (p. 17). To use the "language of the holy book" to celebrate the genealogy of a horse perhaps suggests an ironization of the familiar conceit that America has "descended" from Jerusalem, but Gamut's genealogy also shows again how comments on generation and questions of descent and origin are almost reflexively affiliated with questions of identity in animals and humans. After these remarks, Gamut leans on his "low, gaunt, switch-tailed mare," "while a foal was quietly making its morning repast, on the opposite side of the same animal" (p. 18), as though the mare fed both. In what looks like an attempt to establish new forms of bodies, the novel repeatedly involves Gamut in a suspicious questioning of generation and descent.

The apparently artificial construction of Gamut's body is emphasized again when he rides into the forest: his body unsurprisingly "possessed the power to arrest any wandering eye," since it appears as an "optical illusion"; "the undue elongation of his legs" produces "such sudden growths and diminishings of his stature as baffled every conjecture that might be made as to his dimensions" (pp. 22, 23). The problem of the unnaturally growing and diminishing dimensions of David's body calls attention to its production as an unsolvable question in geometry. Duncan Heyward asks if he is "one who draws lines and angles, under the pretence of expounding the mathematics" (p. 24) – but it is the lines and angles of Gamut's body that produce mathematical explanation. He claims to "understand not your allusions about lines and angles," but such allusions line up with the artificial production of humans in the wilderness, and may even be seen to produce the intersection between human beings and the forest as a geometrical matter of lines, angles, and figures in the wilderness space. This geometry appears as "an inhabitant of the forest" "traced the route" of

> the light and graceful forms of the females waving among the trees, in the curvatures of their path, followed at each bend by the manly figure of Heyward, until, finally, the shapeless person of the singing master was concealed behind the numberless trunks of trees, that rose in dark lines in the intermediate space. (p. 27)

To describe "females" as "forms," or "numberless trunks of trees" as "dark lines," presents the elements of the wilderness that might appear most natural as an entirely unnatural matter of forms, numbers, "curvatures," and bends. This attention to proportion, geometry, and measure suggests, one might say, an artifactual and almost technological landscape.

Appropriately at home in this landscape is the perpetually discursive Natty Bumppo, who stops dangerously during the suspense of a gunfight to give a lecture about his rifle: "'Of all we'pons,' he commenced, 'the long barrelled, true grooved, soft metalled rifle, is the most dangerous in skillful hands, though it wants a strong arm, a quick eye and great judgment in charging to put forth all its beauties'" (p. 70). His elaborate attention to the proportions and dimensions of the killing machine in the wilderness suggests the technology of the machinery of death generally in the novel. Such a mechanics of death appears, for instance, as "the tomahawk of Heyward, and the rifle of Hawk-eye, descended on the skull of the Huron, at the same moment that the knife of Uncas reached his heart" (p. 113). Again, this overkill indicates the emblematic status of a dehumanized violence which Natty Bumppo presents with an affection for the personified machinery of that violence. "'I have got back my old companion, "kill-deer,"' he added, striking his hand on the breech of his rifle" (p. 116).

A different loss of distinction between animal and human, taking the form of an "unfitness between sound and sense" (p. 27), is exacerbated when the inhabitants of the cave at Glen's Falls listen to the screams of the frightened horses and think they hear something supernatural – or, almost equivalently, Indians – or "a sort of unhuman sound." "I did believe there was no cry that Indian or beast could make, that my ears had not heard," comments Natty (p. 59). "I have listened to all the sounds of the woods for thirty years. . . . There is no whine of the panther; no whistle of the cat-bird; nor any invention of the devilish Mingoes, that can cheat me! I have heard the forest moan like mortal men in their affliction" (p. 62). Bringing together animals, forest, invention, and "mortal men," Natty Bumppo calls attention to the possibility of a "cheat," or of the artificial construction of identity in the wilderness. The blurring of boundaries between animal and human in this wilderness comes increasingly to accompany such artifice or cheating, especially through disguise, and specifically through the taking on of animal identities. These deliberate transgressions at once infuse agency into the inanimate (the forest can "moan like mortal men") and withdraw agency from inhabitants of the forest; whether made by "Indian or beast," what Natty Bumppo listens for is the "sounds of the woods."

The novel's merging of persons and landscapes first appears when the travelers enter the woods through a "blind path [that] became visible" (p. 21).[9] Although the immediate question for the travelers is whether they can see the path, the play on blindness and visibility, and the suggestion that the natural world might be able to see them as well, if it were not "blind," is part of the more general animism that appears in Cooper's landscapes. Such a possibility gets raised repeatedly about inanimate objects in the woods, and in consequence problems about animation and agency in the novel tend to be correlated with problems of vision and visibility. Duncan Heyward, for example, looking about him after he has led them into this blind path, "believed he had mistaken some shining berry of the woods, for the glistening eyeballs of a prowling savage" (p. 27). But eyes are often taken for unseeing things in the forest. In making berries and "eyeballs" appear the same, the passage both removes agency from the "prowling savage" by seeing an eyeball as a "shining berry" and ascribes agency to the woods by imagining its shining berries capable of vigilance. A perhaps more conventional example of Heyward's deluded sight occurs in the following scene:

> Glancing his eyes around, with a vain attempt to pierce the gloom that was thickening beneath the leafy arches of the forest, [Heyward] felt as if, cut off from human aid, his unresisting companions would soon lie at the entire mercy of those barbarous enemies, who, like beasts of prey, only waited till the gathering darkness. . . . His awakened imagination, deluded by the deceptive light, converted each wavering bush, or the fragment of some fallen tree, into human forms. (p. 45)

Although Duncan converts bushes and trees into human form, the "human forms" he imagines are "like beasts of prey." These distinctions among human, animal, and vegetable "forms" become critically difficult to maintain as he produces a radically animated landscape.

93

This uncertain crossing of human and nonhuman elements of the landscape produces other difficulties with identification. When Duncan, hiding near the Indian camp later in the novel, sees a clearing where a "hundred earthen dwellings stood on the margin of the lake," he thinks that their "rounded roofs . . . denoted more of industry and foresight than the natives were wont to bestow on their regular habitations." Looking out for the "natives" who inhabit the landscape, he finds himself surprised by their unnatural industry: "In short, the whole village, or town, which ever it might be termed, possessed more of method and neatness of execution, than the white men had been accustomed to believe belonged, ordinarily, to the Indian habits." The "method and neatness" that determine the outlines of the "town" are not the only aesthetic features of the landscape that surprise this white man; the houses are beneath a "cataract so regular and gentle, that it appeared rather to be the work of human hands, than fashioned by nature" (p. 218). Even to see a waterfall as "fashioned by nature" comes close to presenting it as an unnatural construction, but to see it as the "work of human hands" leads to a further blunder about the native builders who construct the landscape. Although Duncan "fancied he discovered several human forms, advancing towards him on all fours" until "the place seemed suddenly alive with beings" (p. 219), he is startled to discover at last that these "forms" or "beings" are industrious beavers.

Almost as revealing as Duncan's failure to see, or failure to distinguish, the difference between "human forms" and animal, between the safe site of a beaver dam and the dangerous homes of Indians, is his subsequent racial identification of a human form, which continues this series of generic mislabelings. Near the beaver dam, he sees a "stranger Indian" whose facial features cannot be discovered "through the grotesque masque of paint, under which they were concealed" (p. 219). Completing a series of transformations among animal, human, and Indian, this form is unmasked as David Gamut, who has been disguised by the Hurons holding him captive. Duncan's superficial scrutiny appears as an almost willful refusal to distinguish between forms and disguises: "His lurking Indians were suddenly converted into four-footed beasts; his lake into a beaver pond; his cataract into a

94

dam . . . and a suspected enemy into his tried friend" (p. 222). To convert Indians into "four-footed beasts," and confuse the boundaries between human and nonhuman constructions, or to transpose animal identities with human ones becomes continuous with substituting Indian for white identities. In addition, for Duncan to see Gamut as an Indian suggests that all the white man needs to take on an Indian identity is to be painted, as though the capacity of whites to improvise a racial identity consisting of superficial marks and remaining at the surface of the skin were set in contrast with the fixed racial identity of the Indian. Indeed, Duncan himself gets painted as an Indian and follows Gamut back to the Indian camp after this lesson in how to change racial identity.[10]

Leaving behind the beaver dam with "those little huts, that he knew were so abundantly peopled," and coming to the "margin of another opening, that bore all the signs of having been also made by the beavers," Duncan discovers "some fifty or sixty lodges, rudely fabricated of logs, brush, and earth":

> They were arranged without any order, and seemed to be constructed with very little attention to neatness or beauty. Indeed, so very inferior were they, in the latter two particulars, to the village Duncan had just seen, that he began to expect a second surprise, no less astonishing than the former. This expectation was in no degree diminished, when, by the doubtful twilight, he beheld twenty or thirty forms, rising alternately from the cover of the tall, coarse grass in front of the lodges, and then sinking again from the sight, as it were to burrow in the earth. (p. 230)

This "second surprise" does seem rather "less astonishing" than the first because it involves what would no longer be surprising, and indeed has become an "expectation": seeing animals where Indians were anticipated, or, in this case, seeing an Indian camp as inferior to a beaver's. This expectation is enhanced by the materials with which both Indians and beavers build their villages: both have "earthen dwellings" as though the natural shelter or burrow of both of these forms were the earth itself, or even as though little distinction could be made between earth and the "forms" that burrowed in it, whether human or animal. Watching the "juvenile pack" of the Indian camp, for example, Duncan finds that the "naked, tawny bodies of the crouching urchins, blended so nicely, at that hour, with the withered herbiage, that at first it seemed as if the earth had, in truth, swallowed up their forms" (p. 232). But of course a distinction is made: the artistic deficiencies of the Indian village, where Duncan looks for arrangement and human "order," "neatness," and "beauty," are presented as "inferior" to the "method and neatness of execution" of the beaver dam. Such distinctions are certainly part of a familiar scheme in which a white author both mythologizes and denigrates Native Americans, but they also work to produce an emphatically uncertain relation between human and nonhuman, the cultural and the natural.

The identities of Indian and beaver are collapsed again when Chingachgook improbably disguises himself as a beaver and hides from the Hurons in the same beaver dam that has just confused Duncan Heyward. The beaver has a particular symbolic resonance for the Hurons in this novel. Magua, for example, uses the beaver to initiate a hierarchy of discriminations between humans and animals, Indians and white, by claiming that "wisdom" is the quality that provides the "great point of difference between the beaver and other brutes; between brutes and men; and, finally, between the Hurons, in particular, and the rest of the human race" (p. 282). When the Hurons pass Chingachgook's hiding place, the beavers are addressed by "one chief of the party who carried the beaver as his particular symbol, or 'totem' [and] called the animals his cousins" (p. 284).[11] The Hurons take it as a sign of "gratifying the family affection of the warrior," when they see the "head of a large beaver . . . thrust from the door of a lodge." But the family affection that the Huron warrior experiences with the beaver's head turns out to be an identification with a human interloper. A transmutation occurs when the warriors leave: "Had any of the Hurons turned to look behind them, they would have seen . . . the entire animal issue from the lodge, uncasing, by the act, the grave features of Chingachgook from his mask of fur" (p. 285). Changing species identity by donning a fur mask, Chingachgook seems perversely to enforce the associations that Duncan makes between Indians and animals. More significantly, for Indians as well as whites in this novel, identity can appear a matter of surface and artifice.

The effects of looking for identity on the surface of the skin are

displayed when Duncan, disguised as an Indian healer and search-
ing for Alice in an Indian cave, confronts what he believes to be a
bear. The "fierce and dangerous brute . . . turned and came wad-
dling up to Duncan, before whom it seated itself, in its natural
attitude, erect like a man" (p. 256). The reason why the "natural
attitude" of the bear includes erect posture "like a man" may well
be because it *is* a man, dressed as a bear, so that it is at once
"natural" for it to sit "erect like a man," and a sign of good artifice
that a man dressed as a bear can appear as "natural" as the bear
who sits "like a man." Cooper's apparent source for this scene,
John Heckewelder, writes similarly about a conjurer disguised as a
bear: "'a human being to transform himself so as to be taken for a
bear walking on his hind legs?' . . . the more he went on with his
performance, the more I was at a loss to decide, whether he was a
human being or a bear; for he imitated that animal in the greatest
perfection, walking upright on his hind legs as I had often seen it
do. . . . [H]e assured me that although outside it had the appearance of a bear, yet inside there was a man."[12] Heckewelder
needs assurance in order to keep the distinction between the outside appearance of the bear and the inside presence of the man. His
anxiety suggests that the problem of "imitating that animal to
perfection" is the "loss" of the presence of the human being, such
that imitation *becomes* transformation, and the outside "appearance" displaces the "inside" man.[13]

When Natty Bumppo unmasks himself, Duncan compliments
him on his performance: "the animal itself might have been
shamed by the representation" (p. 257). The "scout" happily ex-
plicates:

> "Had it now been a catamount, or even a full-sized painter, I would
> have embellished a performance, for you, worth regarding! But it is
> no such marvellous feat to exhibit the feats of so dull a beast;
> though, for that matter too, a bear may be over acted! Yes, yes; it is
> not every imitator that knows natur may be outdone easier than she
> is equalled." (257–8)

Natty Bumppo's skill in embellishing the performance of the bear,
the restraint he announces in equalling but not exceeding "natur,"
calls attention to the bear's identity *as* a performance. In Duncan's
suggestion that Natty's representation would shame the "animal

itself," however, Cooper seems to propose that the observing bear, "erect like a man," would, like the observing human, be "at a loss to decide, whether he was a human being or a bear." Like Chingachgook, Natty Bumppo transforms himself with the skin of another species in a manner that challenges the integrity of species distinctions. Taking the skin of another species to save his own skin challenges natural and cultural distinctions in such a way that the idea of the natural becomes bound up with representation, acting, and imitation.

These artificial transformations between human and animal states may stand in for the struggle between Indians and whites over land and identity, and in the next section I will consider how the crossings of racial and human boundaries become affiliated with a specifically racialized and gendered formation of national culture. For the moment I want to focus on how the novel makes it obtrusively difficult to decipher or classify identity – a difficulty appearing most obviously in the multiple disguises of characters – and how it insistently refuses to assign precise racial, national, or biological identity. It can even paradoxically seem that the novel's very insistence on rigid categories and classifications, or on actions justified by such categories, calls them into question.

In her discussion of *The Last of the Mohicans*, Jane Tompkins claims that by "putting on a disguise none of the characters risks his or her own identity." That is, she finds identity, finally, a determinate property. But the disguises and substitutions of the novel indicate a more fundamental uneasiness about the constructedness of identity, or about whether the body is more than a theater for the performance of identity. Rather than showing, as Tompkins argues, a "proper respect for the 'natural' divisions that separate tribe from tribe and nation from nation," *The Last of the Mohicans* repeatedly makes such divisions at once unnatural and violently contested. Tompkins astutely suggests that the novel's "subject is cultural miscegenation," but insists at the same time that it works to restore order by working against that miscegenation, since "what is to be avoided, in short, is . . . the confusion of mutually exclusive systems of classification, which is what occurs when disparate cultures collide with one another."[14] As we have seen, however, rather than working to avoid "mutually exclusive sys-

tems of classification," the novel obsessively reiterates such collisions and confusions in its very production of identity, and, further, produces identities by a miscegenation of animal and human,
natural and cultural.

Disguises in the novel involve a cultural miscegenation or blend-
ing of human and animal orders through elaborate and even far-
cical concealments of the human body – in a bear costume, say, or
in a beaver dam.[15] The pathos of being born into a racially hier-
archical culture is played out and ratified through disguise and
substitution and through shifting biological or racial identities
within that culture. When, for example, Duncan Heyward and
Natty Bumppo, disguised respectively as an Indian healer and a
bear, go into the Indian cave to rescue Alice, they must first con-
front an ill Huron woman they have ostensibly come to cure. The
Indian woman "lay in a sort of paralysis, . . . happily unconscious
of suffering," and Duncan finds that his "slight qualm of conscience" about the "deception" of being a "pretended leech" is
"instantly appeased" by her unconsciousness (p. 253). They carry
Alice out of the cave disguised as the Indian woman, who, left
alone in the cave, dies. Natty Bumppo instructs Duncan to "wrap
[Alice] in them Indian cloths. Conceal all of her little form. Nay,
that foot has no fellow in the wilderness; it will betray her. All,
every part" (p. 259). To rescue Alice, they wrap her in "them
Indian cloths," another version of giving her the skin of a different
identity. The rescue of the white woman is made possible by, and
even seems to be paid for by, the death of the Indian woman they
leave behind in the cave. The novel might be said to locate the
future of national culture in the wrapping of Alice's body – and in
the activities of Duncan Heyward and Natty Bumppo who wear
the skins of another race but act in that guise to valorize and rescue
their own race. Although characters clearly engage in such disguises and transformations to save their own skins, the prolifera-
tion of these acts troubles the presumed integrity of human or
racial identity. Moreover, in the death of the ill, and apparently
irrelevant, Indian woman abandoned in the cave, and in the saving of Alice, or in the transfer of generative power from the Indian
woman to Alice, we may locate the question of how both history
and generation are acted out on the bodies of women, that is,

those who can transmit identity. It is this enactment of genera-tional and historical continuity to which I want to turn.

In the 1826 preface to the novel, Cooper refuses pleasure to the "reader, who takes up these volumes, in expectation of finding an imaginary and romantic picture" (p. 1). Insisting on the conven-tional disclaimer of the novelist that his "narrative" is based on facts, and demanding that his reader work from the first page to understand the "obscurities of the historical allusions," he warns off those who are "under the impression that it is a fiction" (p. 1). More significantly for our purposes, his rigorous segregation of readers of fact and of fiction depends on an opposition between male and female readers, between the facts fit for the male au-dience of the historian and the desires of the "more imaginative sex, some of whom, under the impression that it is a fiction, may be induced to buy the book" (p. 1). Cooper wants to "advise all young ladies,"[16] "if they have the volumes in hand, with intent to read them, to abandon the design" because they "will surely pro-nounce it shocking" (p. 4).

What is the shock that the "more imaginative sex" will experi-ence as a result of reading *The Last of the Mohicans?* Perhaps it is the shock that William Cobbett so graphically described a few years earlier in the preface to his political pamphlet *A Bone to Gnaw for the Democrats:* "If you are of that sex, vulgarly called the fair, . . . let me beseech you, if you value your charms, to proceed no further." Warning women to desist from reading (and writing), he presents a fearful precedent: "have we not a terrible example of recent, very recent date? I mean that of the unfortunate *Mary Wollstoncraft* [sic]. It is a well known fact, that, when that political lady began *The Rights of Women,* she had as fine black hair as you would wish to see, and that, before the second sheet of her work went to the press, it was turned as white, and a great deal whiter than her skin." Thus comparing Mary Wollstonecraft, whose hair turns whiter than her skin, and, perhaps, as white as the "sheet of her work," while writing about the politics of women's rights, with the reader who will lose her "charms" from reading about politics, Cobbett concedes that "It is a little singular for an author to write a Preface to hinder his work from being read; but this is not my intention; all I wish to do, is, to confine it within its proper sphere."[17] His separation of reading spheres, like Cooper's, becomes a separation of gender spheres. As women are warned not to read Cobbett's political work since it will cause their bodies to change unnaturally, so are they also warned from inhabiting Cooper's historical space. This political and historical exclusion of women as writers and readers may relate to the novel's representation of women as characters, and, beyond that, the novel's elimination of women, and women's bodies, from the sphere of history and its making.

Warding off women readers generally, the novel more specifically displays an anxiety about mothers, and what appears, finally, to be an anxiety about natural reproduction. For one thing, there is the notion popularized during the American Revolution that England, as a mother, has failed the colonies, as children. National identity in the newly formed United States is built on simultaneously emphasizing and repudiating England's role as a mother.[18] In the historical explanation with which he opens the novel, Cooper presents what has already become a national mythology when he states that the colonies have been "reverencing" England "as a mother" they "had blindly believed invincible" (p. 13). To see England as a mother who is now "vincible" is to see motherhood, at least that nation as mother, as something that can be overcome. By this reading, the birth of a nation comes not from recognizing but from repudiating that mother, or from repudiating the nation-as-mother in order to produce a kind of self-making appropriate in a nation of self-made and celibate men, men such as Natty Bumppo. Looking to England for protection, the colonies find she has failed to provide for their safety. On the frontier, "mothers cast anxious glances" at their children (p. 13), anxious because of the Indian threat England is supposed to be protecting them from. They should perhaps be more anxious about the violence the novel has in store for them. Indeed, *all* mothers are eliminated from the novel, or, as with the mothers of Cora and Alice and Uncas, dispatched beforehand.

This violence against mothers is part of the violence against natural reproduction or against the natural family. The violence that the novel directs against Cora and Alice and Uncas, for example, seems motivated by their status as children. As the "last of the Mohicans," Uncas is at once the last child and the last possibility of a new generation. The attempts Alice and Cora make to get to their father are thwarted because Magua sees them as standing in for their father. (It is, of course, the thwarted journey of daughters to father and, in the second half of the novel, of father to daughters, that produces the novel's plot.) When Magua proposes to Cora, he does not address her by name, but calls her "the daughter of the English chief" and "the daugher of Munro" (p. 104).[19] Such a relation to the identity of the parent reminds us that, as a female child, Cora has inherited at once a racial and a national identity and can transmit these identities. "Like thee and thine," says Cora to the old Indian chief Tamenund, "the curse of my ancestors has fallen heavily on their child!" (p. 305). The novel repeatedly links an inherited identity with the violence directed against its biological carriers: women and children.[20]

These links appear vividly in Horatio Greenough's "Rescue Group" (1853), a statue that stood on the front steps of the national Capitol well into the twentieth century: A mother and child cower beneath the raised tomahawk of a fierce Indian. Behind him a gigantic frontiersman grasps the Indian's tomahawk-wielding hand. The statue presents a painfully clear version of how the woodsman must kill the Indian because of the threat the Indian poses to mother and child and an all too familiar justification for exterminating the Indian because he threatens the white family. But while the frontiersman looks down into the eyes of the Indian who looks back up at him, the extended line of sight of the frontiersman suggests that his eyes look ominously down at the mother huddled over her child.[21] In consequence, the towering figure of the frontiersman also seems to threaten the woman and the child, expressing a violence at once mediated and displaced by the violence between men. In this alternative scenario, the frontiersman's threatened violence toward the mother and child is inextricable from the violence directed toward the Indian who threatens them; the Indian seems almost, then, a surrogate victim, at once a threat to, and a substitute for, the family.

In the massacre scene at the middle of *The Last of the Mohicans*, no rescuing hand stays the Indian tomahawk and the mother and child are killed. Although his sources for the Massacre emphasize that the Indians initially killed wounded soldiers, Cooper chooses instead to focus on a "mass of women and children" that he compares to "alarmed and fluttering birds."[22] Specifically, in a scene that mimics the more involved kidnappings of the novel, a "wild and untutored Huron" offers to trade a woman's baby for her worldly goods. When she does not adequately meet his ransom demands, the "savage" "dashed the head of the infant against a rock" and "mercifully drove his tomahawk into her own brain" (p. 175).[23] Initiating a massacre by killing a mother and child, he kills both the next generation and the source of that generation.

Because Magua has other designs on Cora and Alice, he saves them from the subsequent slaughter of women and children. Renewing his proposal to Cora, he announces, "the wigwam of the Huron is still open. Is it not better than this place?" (p. 177). In offering Cora his "soiled hand," Magua offers her the chance to escape being sacrificed because of her sex and race, but his offer is inseparable from a violence at once racial and sexual. When Cora repulses Magua, he confronts her with his bloody, "reeking hand," and boasts that "[i]t is red, but it comes from white veins!" (p. 178). The gruesome mixture he invokes of red skin, red blood, and "white veins" appears as a miscegenation made visible, a violent mingling of red skin and white blood. And the choice Magua offers Cora between "this place," a battlefield turned killing field where such miscegenation of red and white occurs, and the "wigwam of the Huron," appears as a choice between rival forms of racial and sexual violence.

Violent miscegenation, or mixing of blood, takes an even more startling form on the battlefield: "The flow of blood might be likened to the outbreaking of a torrent; and as the natives became heatened and maddened by the sight, many among them even kneeled to the earth, and drank freely, exultingly, hellishly, of the crimson tide" (p. 176). Kneeling to the earth and drinking blood, the savages treat the "crimson tide" of the female bodies they have killed as though it were a wilderness stream that nourished them: a hellish generation through violence. the bloodbath moves beyond graphic descriptions of battles into an emblematic and terrifying fantasy of the "unnatural" mixing of blood in which the

Indians violently reproduce miscegenation by killing. In this last and most appalling version of miscegenation we can locate the extreme form that the fear of women and natural reproduction takes in this novel: the crossing of white and red bodies in a nonsexual miscegenation, a drinking of blood. This unnatural mixing of blood provides a final instance of the crossing of boundaries that the novel proposes, a crossing located, even if only by denial, in the bodies of women.

The killing of women and children during the Massacre, like the killing of the deer and the colt with which the novel begins, seems insufficiently motivated as either Indian revenge or as a sacrifice to the wilderness. Although Cooper tends to bring women and children to the frontier and then violently eliminate them, their deaths do not just mark a ritual sacrifice of or for civilization. Rather, these deaths operate as a kind of generation through violence of relations among landscapes, races, and genders. More specifically, they mark a conflict about what makes up a person, or how persons are made, a conflict played out on the frontier between civilization and wilderness, culture and nature, white and red. This conflict appears most dramatically in the anxious representations of women, and of the female body, as conflicted signs of culture and of nature.

The crossing of the cultural and the natural appears, for instance, in Cora, who wears a veil to hide both her "not brown" face and the "colour of the rich blood, that seemed ready to burst its bounds." Yet "her veil also was allowed to open its folds, and betrayed an indescribable look" when she first sees Magua (p. 19). When Cora blushes, she betrays her "blood," a blood her veil does not conceal and her apparently white skin can scarcely contain. Cora's "indescribable look" has been traced to an instinctive racial affinity with Magua, an affinity with the native body that her "telltale blood" (p. 67) repeatedly reveals. Beyond this, the revelation of her "rich blood" at once establishes Cora's racial identity in terms of her blood and brings that racial embodiment together with the female blush. Her blush, that is, brings together her race and her sex, the racial body and the gendered body.

Rather than concealing her identity, Cora's veil, like her blush, reveals her gender and her race. Her veil arouses attention in the forest, enabling Uncas and the others to track her from the massacre scene when they notice she has dropped "the rag she wore to hide a face that all did love to look upon" (p. 185). For Cora to hide her face seems another version of the concealments and disguises that proliferate in the novel. If her veil fails to "hide a face that all did love to look upon," however, as her skin barely contains her blood, both female face and racial blood are paradoxically revealed through and by means of veil and skin. Veil and skin, artifact and body thus work together as the nature and culture of Cora's racial and sexual identity.

Cora's veil, left behind in the forest, echoes "those dense shadows, that seemed to draw an impenetrable veil before the bosom of the forest" (p. 47). Moreover, the veil that "covers" for her identity permits a chain of relations between landscapes and the female body that returns us to the question of the relation between the female body and the nature of the Native American. Gendered by veil and bosom both, the forest appears female and even maternal, yet the "impenetrable veil" that the shadows draw across that bosom suggests also an uneasy relation between such a maternal personification of the forest and the threat its dense shadows pose. The threat behind the veil appears dramatically when the travelers initially enter the woods and the "forest at length appeared to swallow up the living mass which had slowly entered its bosom" (p. 15). Converting persons into a "living mass," and the bosom of the forest into a kind of mouth that swallows them, this passage makes the female or maternal forest into an ominous consumer of humans.

Such a contradictory or conflicted image of the female body draws gender, race, and landscape into contested relations. Cooper's presentation of the forest as a maternal body that swallows rather than delivers human bodies inverts the more familiar relation between the maternal earth and Indian bodies that his sources depicted. "The Indians consider the earth as their universal mother," notes Heckewelder. "They believe that they were created within its bosom." Before their birth from the bosom of the earth, they "contend that their existence was in the form of certain terrestrial animals." The genealogy of this earlier animal embodi-

105

ment and this relationship to a personified mother earth produces a belief in the "intimate ties of connexion and relationship" that exist "between man and the brute creation." The Indians, according to Heckewelder, do not classify the difference between animals and humans in the way that whites do, because in personifying the earth as their mother they include "terrestrial animals" in a family relation.

To structure the genealogy of human identity in this way, to find human identity continuous with identity as an animal, affects or even structures the grammar of the Indian language, according to Heckewelder. Specifically, rather than differentiating in terms of gender, the Indians Heckewelder describes discriminate by the animate and the inanimate: "Hence, in their languages, these inflections of their nouns which we call *genders,* are not, as with us, descriptive of the *masculine* and *feminine* species, but of the *animate* and *inanimate* kinds."[24] For the grammar of the presumably white "us" that Heckewelder addresses, gender discriminations exist as species discriminations, and it seems almost as though to have a masculine or feminine identity is to belong to a distinct species. In contrast, the discrimination between the animate and the inanimate not only softens distinctions of gender but also aligns animate "kinds," suggesting a continuity among human, wilderness, and animal identities.

These complicated relations among, for example, veil and blood as signs of female and racial identity, and the uneasy tensions among landscapes, animals, and persons, reappear in the novel as a problem of language, and specifically as the problematic involvement of women with reading and writing. Natty Bumppo resentfully notes that "a man who is too conscientious to spend his days among the women, in learning the names of black marks, may never hear of the deeds of his fathers" (p. 31). In this association between women and language, women are the source of "the names of black marks" which carry "the deeds of his fathers." Natty resists women, in this view, both as linguistic transmitters of a patriarchal identity and as biological carriers of that identity.

The relationship between women and language appears in yet another guise in Cooper's preface: He describes how the Lenape, laying aside their arms, become "in the figurative language of the natives, 'women' " (p. 3). Natty Bumppo notes, "I have heard that the Delawares have laid aside the hatchet, and are content to be called women!" (p. 50). In the sources Cooper drew on, to be called women is to have stopped fighting and to act as negotiators for peace. The Delaware are pressured "to assume that station by which they would be the means, and the only means, of . . . saving the Indian race from utter extirpation." Faced with such pressure to save the race by changing gender, "to become *the woman* in name . . . they gave their consent and agreed to become *women*."[25] Like the taking on of animal identities, this transmutation involves both imitation and a kind of transformation. To become nominally a woman is a choice made in the name of or in order to rescue racial and national identity, but, at least for the white observer, it also implicates the Indian nation in a suspicious identification with female gender.[26] And it raises again the question of how national identity gets transmitted: through blood or through the name, through deeds of the fathers or women's naming of the fathers.

In a recent and influential account of national identities, Benedict Anderson argues that "from the start the nation was conceived in language, not in blood." That is, ostensibly natural elements like race and gender are subsumed under the cultural element of language so that "one could be invited into the imagined community. Thus today, even the most insular nations accept the principle of *naturalization.*" Language makes it possible to produce artificially a national identity that seems natural.[27] But Cooper's account indicates a tenser relation between the natural and linguistic "conceptions" of the nation and indicates further, through the chain of associations among genders and races, and how they are mapped onto landscapes and languages, that the project of national formation cannot be separated from these competing forms of bodily and linguistic ways of conceiving a national self. That Cora, for example, has "a blood purer and richer than the rest of her nation" (p. 343) indicates the uncertain crossings of gender, race, and nation. The links between violence against women and violence against Indians, as Greenough's "Rescue Group" suggests, crucially involve relations between national landscapes and the female body, and between the female body and the native race.

107

It may finally be that the danger for women in *The Last of the Mohicans* is that the novel's violence involves, after all, not quite killing a man, but killing a woman, or a man seen in female terms, those who have become woman. Such a reading indicates not just the crossing of racial and female identities, but the elimination or replacement of both by a fantasy of national identity. For Natty Bumppo to be "a man without a cross" in a novel where everything seems to be a matter of crossing the natural and the cultural may even be for him to be a man not born of woman. In Cooper's American project of settling and founding nature, we find such an identity at once naturalized and nationalized.

NOTES

1. I am suggesting that the notion of regeneration through violence points to the work of this ritualized violence but does not quite register the ways in which problems of generation and gender are bound up with these rituals. Richard Slotkin, *Regeneration through Violence: The Mythology of the American Frontier, 1600–1860* (Middletown, Conn.: Wesleyan University Press, 1973).

2. For example: "The foremost Indian bounded like a stricken deer, and fell headlong" (p. 70) or "a Delaware leaping high into the air, like a wounded deer, fell . . . dead" (p. 329). The word "kind," from Middle English "kinde," primarily means "nature, race, origin" (synonyms are order, genus, race). An archaic meaning of gender, however, is also "kind." See Donna Harraway, "Gender for a Marxist Dictionary: The Sexual Politics of a Word," for a discussion of the "gender identity paradigm": "Words close to gender are implicated in concepts of kinship, race, biological taxonomy, language, and nationality." In *Simians, Cyborgs, and Women: The Reinvention of Nature* (New York: Routledge, 1991), p. 130.

3. See Leslie Fiedler on the "scandal" of Cora's mixed blood and Uncas's posthumous marriage with her. Leslie Fiedler, *Love and Death in the American Novel* (New York: Criterion Books, 1960), pp. 204–5.

4. I am indebted to Mark Seltzer for this phrase, and for discussions about some of the topics of this essay. See Mark Seltzer, "The Love-Master," in *Engendering Men*, ed. Michael Cadden and Joseph Boone (New York: Routledge, 1990), pp. 214–34.

5. Drawing on the accounts of this myth by John Heckewelder, who was

Cooper's source for much of his information about the Indians, Richard Slotkin applies the myth to the deer slaying in *The Pioneers* and to Natty Bumppo's acquisition of the name "Deer-slayer." Slotkin, *Regeneration Through Violence,* pp. 46, 306. John Heckewelder, *An Account of the History, Manners, and Customs of the Indian Nations* (Philadelphia: Abraham Small, 1819), p. 251. Slotkin finds this an allegory about the regeneration of a cultural order through the violent absorption of a natural one, but I want to trace the natural as already imbricated with the mark of the cultural. H. Daniel Peck also discusses Heckewelder in *A World By Itself: The Pastoral Moment in Cooper's Fiction* (New Haven: Yale University Press, 1977), p. 126.

6. Indeed, it is the cultural work of rendering inevitable – of lending ideology the invulnerable banality of the hard fact – that his account may be seen at once to examine and to reinforce or conserve. Philip Fisher, *Hard Facts: Setting and Form in the American Novel* (New York: Oxford, 1985).

7. Richard Slotkin, *The Fatal Environment: The Myth of the Frontier in the Age of Industrialization, 1800–1890* (Middletown, Conn.: Wesleyan University Press, 1989), p. 89. Cooper is fond of the neutral territory depicted in *The Spy,* a territory that has been called the land of the American romance, where these distinctions are often violently refigured. The whole action of *The Last of the Mohicans* takes place in disputed territory claimed by the French and English. The Indian claims to the land are made to seem incidental.

8. Gamut's extravagantly constructed body and the treatment he receives seem designed to bring the comic relief of Washington Irving's Ichabod Crane. Like Gamut, Ichabod Crane is

> a native of Connecticut, a state which supplies the Union with pioneers for the mind as well as the forest, and sends forth yearly its legions of frontier woodsmen and country schoolmasters. . . . He was tall, but exceedingly lank, with narrow shoulders, long arms and legs, hands that dangled a mile out of his sleeves, feet that might have served for shovels, and his whole frame most loosely hung together.

Crane's talent is also like Gamut's: the "singing-master of the neighborhood," his voice, with its "peculiar quavers," "resounded far above all the rest." Washington Irving, "Legend of Sleepy Hollow," in *The Sketch Book* (1820) (New York: New American Library, 1961), pp. 332, 334. For sending forth such notably inept schoolmasters, Connecticut is vilified as the source of an inept model of education and religion. Gamut's profession is singing – "I teach singing to the youths of the Connecticut levy" (p. 57) – but his singing often creates or accompanies danger: He almost always begins in and even precipitates perilous moments. In the cave, his singing is succeeded by and almost blends with the screams of the horses, "that horrid cry" first thought to be supernatural (p. 60).

9. Their entry into the woods is also sexualized as they approach a path "which might, with some little inconvenience, receive one person at a time" (p. 21), a "dark and tangled pathway" which they enter by "penetrating the thicket" (p. 22).

10. Natty tells Duncan to wash off his Indian disguise before he sees Alice: "young women of white blood give the preference to their own colour." After he "availed himself of the water," "every frightful or offensive mark was obliterated, and the youth appeared again in the lineaments with which he had been gifted by nature" (p. 258). By this point, to appear in the "lineaments" of his own color seems another choice of disguise. On improvisatory identification as a tactic of power, see Stephen Greenblatt, "Improvisation and Power," *Literature and Society: Selected Papers from the English Institute, 1978* (Baltimore: Johns Hopkins University Press, 1980), pp. 57–8.

11. Cooper may derive his attention to the beaver, "those sagacious and industrious animals," from George Henry Loskiel, a missionary-anthropologist who describes "The *Beaver* of North America," in similarly anthropomorphic terms, commenting on the "amazing sagacity of these animals, displayed in building their dwellings, in their whole economy." George Henry Loskiel, *History of the Mission of the United Brethren Among the Indians in North America,* trans. from the German by Christian La Trobe (London: Brethren's Society for the Furtherance of the Gospel, 1794), p. 81.

12. Heckewelder, *An Account,* p. 234.

13. A later version of the threat of these transposed positions shows up in "Circumstance" (1860), a story by Harriet Prescott Spofford about a woman caught in the grasp of a panther known as the "Indian devil." The woman is terrified of being eaten because her body would continue to exist inside a creature who threatens her both as a beast and as a stand-in for the Indian. Edgar Huntly acts out a reversal of the ingestion of both flesh and qualities when he eats the panther he finds in the cave in Charles Brockden Brown's *Edgar Huntly.* To eat the body of the panther that threatened his life seems a more direct version of Richard Slotkin's concept of internalizing the wilderness in order to rejuvenate the culture that presents itself as opposed to it.

The instances I am treating here of disguise and transposition seem related but act in thematically and politically different ways. Harriet Prescott Spofford, "Circumstance," reprinted in *Provisions*, ed. Judith Fetterley (Bloomington: Indiana University Press, 1986); Charles Brockden Brown, *Edgar Huntly, or Memoirs of a Sleep-Walker* (New York: Penguin, 1988), p. 160.

14. Jane Tompkins, *Sensational Designs: The Cultural Work of American Fiction* (New York: Oxford University Press, 1985), pp. 116, 118, 117. Although I agree with her point that "an obsessive preoccupation with systems of classification – the insignia by which race is distinguished from race, nation from nation, human from animal, male from female – dominates every aspect of the novel," I argue with her conclusion that the novel works to reassert "'natural' divisions" (p. 105).

15. The most absurd mixture of disguises and substitutions may be the rescue of Uncas from the Huron camp which involves Natty Bumppo, who has been disguised as the bear, disguising himself as David Gamut, Uncas disguising himself as the bear, and David Gamut remaining behind in the Indian camp poorly disguised as Uncas.

16. And "all clergymen." See Ann Douglas for this identification of the audience of women novel-readers and a clergy who "might be better employed" (p. 4). *The Feminization of American Culture* (New York: Alfred A. Knopf, 1977). For a recent account of Cooper's use of history in the novel, see Ian Steele, "Cooper and Clio: The Sources for 'A Narrative of 1757,'" *Canadian Journal of American Studies* (Winter 1989): 121–35.

17. William Cobbett, *A Bone to Gnaw for the Democrats* (Philadelphia, 1795), pp. 3–4. I do not want to ignore the possibility that both of these prefaces could be read as provocation, as an invitation to read a forbidden text that sets out to create a Pandora-like desire in the female reader. But I think that reading them as invitation does not change the way these prefaces ward off women. They also work as a curious reversal of the warnings for women, especially young ones, to be wary of novel reading.

18. Associations between families and a national genealogy line up imperfectly, since citizens are not children and the nation not a family, yet the analogy repeatedly appears in the early republic to present the family as a model or a metaphor for the nation, or as a form of explanation, an agent, or an instrument to make political and historical change seem natural. Jay Fliegelman scrutinizes the status of this analogy and how it works to structure political language in *Prodigals*

and Pilgrims: The American Revolution Against Patriarchal Authority (New York: Cambridge University Press, 1982). See also my "Plague and Politics in 1793: *Arthur Mervyn*," *Criticism* (Summer 1985), 225–46. Heckewelder tells how the American Revolution was explained to the Native American: "Disputes having arisen between Great Britain and her North American colonies, and a congress being chosen by the latter, it appointed commissioners, . . . for the purpose of explaining the nature of the dispute to them" (p. 136). After telling them not to get involved, "they next proceeded to state the cause from whence the dispute had originated, calling the same a family dispute, a quarrel between a parent and his child." The Indians pledged that "they would remain neutral during the 'contest between the parent and the son'" (p. 140). A new war chief of the Delawares reinterpreted the scenario: "'You see a great and powerful nation divided! You see the father fighting against the son, and the son against the father' . . . 'At first I looked upon it as a family quarrel . . . at length it appeared to me, that the father was in the right; and his children deserved to be punished a little' . . . from the many cruel acts his offspring had committed from time to time, on his Indian Children" (pp. 216–17).

19. Magua even sees Cora as a dismembered piece of her father's body: He follows up his proposal by saying that while Munro would "sleep among his cannon, his heart would be within reach of the knife of le Subtil" (p. 105). In a more conventional version of declaring a new family allegiance through marriage, when Duncan proposes to marry Alice he asks Munro for the "honour of being your son" (p. 157).

20. Much of the violence of Cooper's novel is directed against a potentially redemptive future generation. The Indian woman who dies in the cave, for example, is introduced as "the wife of one of my bravest young men" (p. 256). Philip Fisher notes that violence against women in Cooper tends to prevent marriages and that the "many unaccomplished marriages tend to thin out the future in advance" (*Hard Facts*, pp. 56–8).

21. I am basing my analysis on the lines of sight that show up in a photograph reproduced by Richard Drinnon; the statue was removed from the Capitol in 1958. See Richard Drinnon, *Facing West: The Metaphysics of Indian-Hating and Empire-Building* (Minneapolis: University of Minnesota, 1980), pp. 131–3.

22. Cooper's several sources included Jonathan Carver, who wrote as a witness to the Massacre, and Humphreys' *Life of Putnam*, which is even more graphic about the bodies of slaughtered women left be-

hind. Jonathan Carver, *Travels Through the Interior Parts of North-America, in the Years 1766, 1767, and 1768* (London, 1778). These and other sources are discussed on pp. 361–5 of the "Explanatory Notes" to the State University of New York Press edition of *The Last of the Mohicans.*

23. The passage echoes the danger posed in "The Distresses of a Frontier Man," Crèvecoeur's classic description of frontier violence in which he imagines that "it is necessary for the good of Britain that my children's brains should be dashed against the walls of the house." Hector St. John de Crèvecoeur, *Letters from an American Farmer* (New York: New American Library, 1963), p. 201.

24. Heckewelder, pp. 249, 254. The whites make a different connection, as we have seen, between human and animal identities, in which they categorize the Indians as beasts. In his other work, Heckewelder cites an Indian chief who looks forward to a time "when your own descendants will testify against you! – will say: we were taught by our parents to believe this! – we were told when we had killed an Indian, that we had done a *good* act! – had killed a wild beast, &c." (p. xi). He inveighs against "a rabble, (a class of people generally met with on the frontiers) who maintained, that to kill an Indian was the same as killing a bear" (p. 130). John Heckewelder, *Narrative of the Mission of the United Brethren Among the Delaware and Mohegan Indians from its Commencement in the Year 1740 to the Close of the Year 1808 . . . by John Heckewelder who was many Years in Service of that Mission* (Philadelphia: McCarty and Davis, 1820).

25. According to one of Cooper's sources, the Iroquois proposed to the Delaware, "One nation shall be the *woman.* We shall place her in the midst and the other nations who make war shall be the man and live around the woman." George Henry Loskiel, *History of the Mission of the United Brethren Among the Indians in North America,* trans. from the German by Christian La Trobe (London: Brethren's Society for the Furtherance of the Gospel, 1794), p. 25. Heckewelder explains that it "must be understood that among these nations wars are never brought to an end but by the interference of the weaker sex. The men, however tired of fighting, are afraid of being considered as cowards if they should intimate a desire for peace." He continues, "They say also that the whites speak too much, and that much talk disgraces man, and is fit only for women," *Account,* pp. 56–7, 58, 189. For Slotkin, in contrast, Cooper "uses sexual analogy to establish the immutability of racial character – nonwhite can become white only to the degree that women can become men" (*Fatal,* p. 90).

26. In his history of the Iroquois, Francis Jennings explains that the "woman" "seems to have meant originally a nation that was assigned a political role of neutrality so as to be able to assume the peacemaker's role when warring tribes wanted to end their strife without losing face. . . . In the mid-eighteenth century the woman metaphor became corrupted by European notions of female subordination, which were wholly at odds with such Iroquois customs as the power of clan matrons to make and unmake chiefs." Francis Jennings, *The Ambiguous Iroquois Empire: The Covenant Chain Confederation of English Colonies* (New York: Norton, 1984), pp. 45–6.

27. Nationalism, according to Benedict Anderson, can be understood by examining "the larger cultural systems that produced it," rather than "self-consciously held political ideologies." Through these cultural systems, but predominantly through language, the means of transmitting cultural systems, "nation-ness" can be "assimilated to . . . all those things one cannot help," such as race and gender. Benedict Anderson, *Imagined Communities: Reflections on The Origin and Spread of Nationalism* (London: Verso, 1983), pp. 19, 131, 133. See Bruno Latour's claim that "there are *acts* of differentiation and identification, not differences and identities (1.1.16). The words 'same and other' are the consequences of trials of strength, defeats and victories. They cannot themselves describe those links." Bruno Latour, *The Pasteurization of France* (Cambridge, Mass.: Harvard University Press, 1988), p. 169. In "The Nazi Myth," Jean-Luc Nancy and Lacoue-Labarthe describe how the notion that national identity can be transmitted through language runs violently into the problem of race: "The race, the people, is linked to *blood*, not to language" (p. 308). Jean-Luc Nancy and Philippe Lacoue-Labarthe, "The Nazi Myth," *Critical Inquiry* 16 (1990): 291–312.

6

The Lesson of the Massacre at Fort William Henry

ROBERT LAWSON-PEEBLES

THE date was August 10, 1757. On the preceding day Lieutenant Colonel George Monro of the British 35th Regiment had signed the terms of capitulation at Fort William Henry. The Fort, at the southern point of Lake George, had been besieged for six days by a mixed force of French, Canadians, and Indians commanded by Louis Joseph Gorzon de Saint-Véran, Marquis de Montcalm. Outnumbered by some five to one and with rapidly depleting ammunition, Monro had asked Major-General Daniel Webb at Fort Edward for reinforcements. Webb had refused assistance and advised Monro to surrender. His letter fell into Montcalm's hands. The French nobleman immediately sent a flag of truce to Monro, repeated his demand that the Fort surrender and, when Monro yet again refused, handed him the letter. Monro saw that his situation was hopeless. In the words of an apparent eyewitness, a Massachusetts officer named Jonathan Carver, "he hung his head in silence, and reluctantly entered into a negotiation."

Monro had little choice. Conditions at the Fort were horrendous. Over three hundred soldiers had been killed or wounded during the siege, and yet more were stricken with smallpox. All the heavier British artillery had been knocked out, and the walls of the Fort had been breached in several places by Montcalm's formidable force of thirty-one cannon and fifteen mortars. The troops of the provincial regiments (drawn from New Jersey and New Hampshire as well as Massachusetts) had already asked Monro to surrender – reasonably, because many of them were accompanied by their wives and families. In these circumstances he obtained the best possible surrender terms. His troops would be allowed "to march out with all the honors of war." They would be given covered wagons to transport their baggage to Fort Edward, and a guard to protect them as they journeyed there. They would even be allowed to retain one six-pounder cannon as a symbol of the bravery of their defense. The major condition was that they should not fight against the French for the next eighteen months. It was a generous and honorable settlement.

As the British forces marched out of the Fort on August 10, however, things began to go wrong. Some of Montcalm's Indians entered the Fort and looted it. The sick who had been left behind were tomahawked in their beds. Then the Indians went in pursuit of the departing British column. The provincial troops and the baggage were at the rear; the Indians plundered the baggage and stripped the troops of their equipment and clothing. Suddenly, according to Carver, "the war whoop was given," and the killing began:

> [M]en, women, and children were dispatched in the most wanton and cruel manner, and immediately scalped. Many of these savages drank the blood of their victims, as it flowed warm from the fatal wound.

The French stood to one side. Their officers continued "discoursing together with apparent unconcern," while a sentinel from whom Carver claimed protection "called me an English dog, and thrust me with violence back again into the midst of the Indians."

Two centuries later, Carver's account might seem rather bloody and biased. It is, however, a model of restraint in comparison with press reports of the Massacre. The story quickly circulated around the provincial newspapers and was reprinted in London journals. The press added its own gory details, and garnished its accounts with xenophobia. Here is *The Pennsylvania Gazette:*

> [T]he French *immediately* after the Capitulation, *most perfidiously,* let their *Indian Blood-Hounds* loose upon our People. . . . The Throats of most, if not all the Women, were cut, their Bellies ripped open, their Bowels torn out and thrown upon the Faces of their *dead* or *dying* Bodies . . . the Children were taken by the Heels, and their Brains beat out against the Trees or Stones, and not one of them saved.

Eventually, Monro collected some of the survivors and marched to Fort Edward. Others less fortunate, like Jonathan Carver, wandered in the woods without food and clothing for several days before reaching safety. Yet others were taken by the Indians northward to Canada, and were never seen again.

Estimates of the carnage vary widely. Carver said that fifteen hundred people were killed or captured. Thomas Mante, a British officer who took part in the war but who certainly was not present at the Massacre, simply said that "about ten or a dozen" men were scalped. The true figure certainly lies between these two extremes. Jeremy Belknap, a careful historian, noted in 1791 that "the New Hampshire regiment happening to be in the rear, felt the chief fury of the enemy. Out of two hundred, eighty were killed and taken." However many were killed, the Massacre made a deep impact. It shattered Monro; Carver noted that "he died in about three months of a broken heart." According to Belknap, the whole of British America was thrown into "the deepest consternation," fueled no doubt by those inflammatory press reports. The incident became part of colonial mythology. In 1822 Timothy Dwight's *Travels* noted that "from that day to the present, it has been familiarly known by the emphatical appellation of the Massacre at Fort William Henry." Some sixty years later, Francis Parkman spent much time and trouble unearthing new evidence and devoted a dozen eloquent pages of *Montcalm and Wolfe* to it.[1]

The Massacre made a deep impact, too, on James Fenimore Cooper, and in *The Last of the Mohicans* he recounted it with some care. He drew on at least four sources: Carver's *Travels* (which he also used for its account of Indian methods of warfare), Benjamin Trumbull's *General History of the United States* (which repeated in detail the newspaper horror stories of braining and disemboweling), David Humphreys' *Life of the Honourable Major General Israel Putnam*, and Dwight's *Travels*. He may also have drawn on personal and local knowledge. He had gone to school at Albany, near the site of Colonel Monro's grave; through his wife he was related to James Delancey, who had been lieutenant governor of the colony of New York in 1757; and he visited the ruins of Fort William Henry shortly before he began the novel.[2]

The mid-1820s must have seemed an appropriate, indeed a compelling, time to write *The Last of the Mohicans*. In 1822 Dwight's *Travels* had recorded a folk memory. Now Dwight's former student wished to perpetuate that memory. (Dwight was President of Yale from 1795 until his death in 1817; Cooper entered Yale in 1803 and was expelled for misconduct in 1805.) Cooper recorded the wish in the novel's subtitle: *A Narrative of 1757.* He published his book in February 1826, almost sixty-nine years after the Massacre, and therefore just within the lifespan allotted by the Bible. His model, Scott's *Waverley* (1814), had similarly looked back at the Jacobite Rebellion of 1745.[3] If anything, Cooper looked back with a stronger sense of history. In the seventh paragraph of *The Last of the Mohicans* he reminded his readers that Washington had played a gallant part in an earlier colonial disaster, General Braddock's defeat at the Battle of the Monongahela (p. 13). The link between the French and Indian War and the Revolution is delicately made, but the delicacy conceals a deadening awareness that the Revolutionary generation and its "moral truth" (p. 13) have almost disappeared – an awareness later sharpened by the coincidental deaths of Jefferson and Adams less than five months after the publication of *The Last of the Mohicans.*[4]

Andrew Delbanco has suggested that Cooper's subject "was nothing less than America's destiny."[5] It may well be that Cooper believed the Massacre played a negative role in shaping that destiny. Certainly, he emphasized its importance by placing it at the literal and metaphorical center of the novel. It occupies Chapter 17 of the novel's 33 chapters, and when (according to the custom of the time) the novel was published in two volumes, it brought the first to an appropriately doomladen close. The events at the Fort, moreover, provide a temporary point of rest between the twin plots of flight and pursuit, and mark the transition from the world of the white races and "history" (as our Eurocentrism defines it) to the Amerindian world of myth, magic, and bewitchment. The events act both as a synecdoche of American history and as a dreadful portent.[6] In the remainder of this essay I will try to explain why, first by setting the Massacre in the context of the legal history of warfare, and second by discussing Cooper's proposed antidote to conflict.

At the beginning of Chapter 18 (and the opening of Volume 2) Cooper attacks the Marquis de Montcalm for "his cruel apathy," and links that attack with an attack on history. Historical accounts, he says, have tended to forget the Massacre, and dwell instead on Montcalm's glorious death when his forces were defeated on the Heights of Abraham in 1759. In consequence, Montcalm is being surrounded by "an atmosphere of imaginary brightness" (p. 180). Cooper is referring here to a controversy over Montcalm's role in the Massacre, that began with the newspaper reports and still has not ended. David Humphreys had said that Montcalm intervened, but to no avail. Thomas Mante went further. He gave a vivid account of the event, spiced with melodrama:

> [A]s soon as the horrid scene commenced, M. de Montcalm exerted his utmost endeavours to put a stop to it. He laid bare his own bosom, and bade them kill their father, but spare the English, who were now under his protection; he even desired the English to defend themselves, and fire on the savages; but the English were seized with such an unaccountable stupor, that they submitted to the tomahawk without resistance; nor were M. de Montcalm's officers idle in the cause of humanity; many of them were wounded in endeavouring to rescue the persons of the English from the barbarous rage of the savages.

Mante raises here a worrying question: Why hadn't the British forces defended themselves? They were, to an extent, still armed. In 1760 Tobias Smollett, writing his *Continuation* of David Hume's *History of England*, had made the same point; and so, too, had Benjamin Trumbull in 1810. Timothy Dwight never considered the question. Indeed, he dismissed all attempts to "exculpate" Montcalm and, in a lengthy and vituperative attack on him, linked the Massacre at William Henry with an earlier one at Fort Oswego. On August 14, 1756 British forces there had surrendered to Montcalm. His Indians had looted the fort and murdered some of the prisoners. According to Dwight, Montcalm had "delivered up twenty of the garrison, in lieu of twenty Indians who had been killed, to be disposed of as these tigers in human shape should think proper." Smollett, who was almost certainly Dwight's source for this incident, agreed that Montcalm bore some responsibility for it, but made no comment on the Frenchman's role at William Henry, where the Indians had repeated "the tragedy of Oswego, with a thousand additional outrages and barbarities."[7]

Although Cooper had different interpretations of the two massacres available to him, he chose to follow the most negative one, Dwight's, without Dwight's excesses of fury. Why should he have done this? Cooper was a noted Francophile, and he would shortly move to France for a number of years. The answer, I think, is to be found in the final paragraph of Chapter 17, when he remarks that

> On every side the captured were flying before their relentless persecutors, while the armed columns of the Christian King stood fast, in an apathy which has never been explained, and which has left an immoveable blot on the, otherwise, fair escutcheon of their leader. (p. 179)

There are two key phrases here. The first is "the Christian King." Montcalm had signed the Articles of Capitulation at William Henry "in the Name of his Most Christian Majesty," that is, Louis XV. The provincial press seized on the phrase: Here is *The Pennsylvania Gazette* again:

> To what a Pitch of Perfidy and Cruelty is the French Nation arrived! Would not an ancient Heathen shudder with Horror, on hearing so hideous a Tale! Is it the *Most Christian King* that could give such Orders? Or could the most savage Nations ever exceed such French Barbarities! Besides this, was it ever known in the Pagan World, that Terms of Capitulation were not held inviolably sacred.

The next issue of the *Gazette* published the Articles in their entirety to prove the point, and the phrase passed into general currency. Tobias Smollett, Thomas Mante, and Joseph Frye, the Colonel of the Massachusetts Regiment, all used it or a variant of it.[8]

The second key phrase is "an immoveable blot on the . . . fair escutcheon." The literal meaning of "escutcheon" is "a shield bearing a coat of arms," thus identifying its owner as a nobleman. Scott used the term in its literal sense in his 1815 novel *Guy Mannering*. From the late seventeenth century, however, the term also took on the metaphorical meaning of "honor" – because shields, due to the changing technology of war, had fallen out of use. In 1697 Dryden coined the phrase "a blot in his escutcheon" to describe the misbehavior of Ovid; and it is from Dryden that Cooper adapts the phrase.[9]

Taken together, the two phrases, occurring in the paragraph that closes Volume 1, make Montcalm the antithesis of Washington, whose description as a Christian hero had opened the volume.

They suggest that Cooper is reflecting on the laws of warfare, which demand that a Christian leader should abide by certain codes of behavior. The laws of warfare are rooted deep in antiquity. By the close of the Middle Ages the chivalric code, with the influence of Roman law and the teaching of the Christian church, had placed a complex series of restraints on the conduct of war. Cooper refers to them when he uses one of Fluellen's Agincourt speeches, from *Henry V,* as an epigraph to one of his chapters:

> Kill the poys and the luggage! 'tis expressly against the law of arms: 'tis as arrant a piece of knavery, mark you now, as can be offered in the 'orld. (p. 318)

Shakespeare, as a supporter of the Tudor succession, is making a prejudiced point against the French. So, it seems, is Cooper. We shall see later on that, in fact, he is doing more than that.[10]

Shakespeare wrote of the law of arms just at the time the law was breaking down. Ordinary people – defined at the time as knaves rather than nobles – were increasingly asked to fight wars. As they were excluded from the chivalric code the result was a growth in bad behavior. The Thirty Years' War (1618–48) provided an extended example of the appalling atrocities that could be committed. It prompted the Dutch lawyer Hugo Grotius (1583–1645) to redefine the laws of warfare. His *Rights of War and Peace,* first published in 1625, set out precise rules elaborated a century and a quarter later by the Swiss jurist Emmerich de Vattel (1714–67). Vattel's *Le droit des gens* was first published in 1758 and translated into English as *The Law of Nations* the following year. The book was very popular on both sides of the Atlantic. Between 1759 and 1838 there were ten English translations, and the work became a standard text in such American colleges as Dartmouth, William and Mary, and Cooper's Yale.[11]

A number of Vattel's rules were simply restatements of Grotius. Women, children, and the sick should not be mistreated. Clemency should be granted to soldiers who surrender. "At a siege," wrote Vattel, "a garrison offering to capitulate are never to be refused their lives." He also added some new rules. The vigor of a defense should not affect the terms of capitulation. "How could it be conceived," he added, "in a knowing [that is, enlightened] age, that it is lawful to punish with death a governor who has defended his place to the last extremity?" Vattel was particularly concerned with the rights of noncombatants, and discussed means of granting them safe conduct. He also recommended the parole system, under which a captured officer could go home and spend his time, as he put it, "with his family," in return promising his captors not to bear arms against them for a specified period.[12]

The Law of Nations was published one year after the Massacre at William Henry, yet it is apparent from the terms of capitulation and from the provincial response to the Massacre that many of Vattel's precepts were already practiced by the warring nations. It is apparent, too, that the plot of Volume 1 of *The Last of the Mohicans,* and Cooper's attack on Montcalm's "cruel apathy," are informed by a detailed awareness of Vattel. Cora and Alice Munro should have been allowed to enter the Fort freely; Montcalm should not have threatened the garrison with Indian reprisals when at first it did not capitulate; none of the horrific events of August 10 should have been allowed to happen. Grotius and Vattel act, as it were, as a silent Greek chorus in the novel. Their standards for wartime behavior were widely respected at the time, and still are to this day. Their influence may be found in the Hague and Geneva Conventions.

There were, however, significant differences between the two jurists, and those differences made Vattel seem all the more important to those who, like Dwight and Cooper, wished to perpetuate the memory of the Massacre. Grotius looked back to the ancients to validate his rules, but Vattel looked around him to establish principles that would be common to all contemporary societies, whatever their differences. Grotius's pages were full of references to Seneca, Livy, Tacitus, and Plutarch. Vattel, in contrast, examined recent European history and aspects of the settlement of America. Grotius sought universality. Vattel was sensitive to the plurality of nations, races, and societies, yet tried to discover laws "which nature has established among all men." He tried to recommend certain common denominators of behavior, and to define the purposes of war. "Unjust motives" for war were "the arrogant desire of command, the ostentation of power, the thirst of riches, the avidity of conquest, hatred, and revenge." Vattel believed in the just war, and in the soldier's right to kill in such a war, but he tried to place limits on violence. As he remarked, in two memorable sentences:

> Let us never forget that our enemies are men. If we are under the disagreeable necessity of prosecuting our right by force of arms, let us not destroy that charity which connects us with all mankind.

Vattel had particular praise for the charity of the British and French. He told, with great approval, an anecdote about the Duke of Cumberland at the Battle of Dettingen (1743). The Duke lay in his tent, his wounds being attended by his surgeon. A French officer was brought in who was more seriously wounded. The Duke immediately instructed his surgeon to attend first to his former enemy.[13] Such anecdotes provided valuable instances of standards of conduct which, in Vattel's view, should be practiced in every society in the world.

Why did Vattel seem so progressive to his contemporaries and the next few generations? There are, I think, two reasons. First, he addressed himself to those changes in the technology of warfare that had caused the term "escutcheon" to move into the realm of metaphor. There had been many developments in firearms, fortifications, and siegecraft. The military, of necessity, became more professional, and a greater value was attached to individual lives, for soldiers were expensive to train and replace. It is to the discredit of Colonel Munro in *The Last of the Mohicans* that he is so besotted with chivalry that he dismisses the forts of Vauban, the famous French engineer, as "scientific cowardice" (p. 161). Such forts were designed to shelter inhabitants from the increasing deadliness of cannon fire. The second, and more important, reason for Vattel's modernity is his pluralism, which can be traced to an earlier writer, Montesquieu. Montesquieu's *L'esprit des lois* was published in 1748, ten years before Vattel's *Le droit des gens,* and it was even more popular, going through ten British editions by 1773. Montesquieu set out an environmentally based analysis of the variety of political and legal relations. Anticipating Vattel, he asserted that

> The law of nations is naturally founded on this principle, that different nations ought in time of peace to do one another all the good

they can, and in time of war as little injury as possible, without prejudicing their real interests.

Clearly, Vattel's translator had Montesquieu in mind when he gave Vattel's text its English title, *The Law of Nations,* and rightly so, for Montesquieu sketched out some of the rules of war that Vattel elaborated on. For instance, Montesquieu distinguished between just and unjust wars. The latter proceeded from "arbitrary principles of glory, convenience, and utility" and they resulted in "torrents of blood."[14]

Between them, Montesquieu and Vattel created an image of a complex, pluralistic world united by a series of sophisticated and humane rules of warfare. The exceptions, wherever they took place, seemed in consequence all the more iniquitous. Vattel had praised the humanity of the Duke of Cumberland at Dettingen, but his troops at the Battle of Culloden (1746) committed so many atrocities that he became known as "the Butcher," even to his friends. Culloden placed a blot on Cumberland's escutcheon that has never been removed, for the name "Butcher" has stuck to him. When Oliver Goldsmith compiled his *History of England* in 1771, he wrote with great distaste about Culloden, and drew the appropriate moral:

> How soever guilty an enemy may be, it is the duty of a brave soldier that he is only to fight an opposer, not a suppliant. The victory was in every respect decisive, and humanity to the conquered would have rendered it glorious. But little mercy was shewn here.[15]

Even less mercy was shown in America. Yet, according to Montesquieu and Vattel, this should not have been the case. Their pluralistic philosophy demanded that their laws work in the New World as well as the Old. Vattel had even addressed himself to the question of colonization. He believed that some areas of Europe had become overpopulated. The Indians, he thought, did not fully occupy the New World. It was therefore reasonable for Europeans to colonize America, but only to the extent of their needs. Vattel praised the first English Puritan settlers and Penn's Quakers for making treaties with the Indians, and for buying from them the land they needed. Unfortunately, his words fell on deaf ears.

Penn's treaty with the Indians became little more than an ideal, celebrated in the Edenic paintings of the Quaker artist Edward Hicks. Wars in America tended to be fought for unjust causes and the result, in Montesquieu's words, was "torrents of blood."

In addition, there was the problem of Indian behavior in battle, about which the European thinkers could not agree. Montesquieu said that, in many respects, the Indians seemed to "understand the rights of war and peace." Vattel was less sure. He suggested that "when the war is with a savage nation, which observes no rules, and never gives quarter," no mercy should be shown so "that by this rigour they might be brought to conform to the laws of humanity." With hindsight, it can be seen that this suggestion was counterproductive. The behavior of all combatants in the French and Indian War was marked by, as Goldsmith put it, "extreme barbarity." Vattel had praised the humanity of British and French soldiers in Europe. Goldsmith, summing up everything that was wrong with the French and Indian War, said that in America "the two nations seemed to have imbibed a part of the savage fury of those with whom they fought, and exercised various cruelties, either from a spirit of avarice or revenge."[16]

Cooper agreed with Goldsmith. The opening two paragraphs of *The Last of the Mohicans* repeat Goldsmith's remarks about the "savage fury" of the war, and reveal Cooper's awareness of Montesquieu and Vattel. This is an unjust war, and it casts a blight across the environment:

> [I]n time, there was no recess of the woods so dark, nor any secret place so lovely, that it might claim exemption from the inroads of those who had pledged their blood to satiate their vengeance, or to uphold the cold and selfish policy of the distant monarchs of Europe. (p. 11)

The conflicts of the protagonists across this "bloody arena" and "fatal region" (p. 12) come to a climax with the account of the Massacre in Chapter 17. It begins with a sentence suggesting that, so far, the battle has been fought in accord with the precepts of Grotius and Vattel: "The hostile armies . . . passed the night of the ninth of August 1757, much in the manner they would, had they encountered on the fairest field of Europe" (p. 167). It ends with

125

"the shrieks of the wounded, and the yells of their murderers"
(p. 179).

As the next chapter opens, the full extent of the blight is portrayed. This is not the fairest field of Europe. The "smouldering ruin" of the Fort is surrounded by hundreds of "stiffening" corpses and, although it is only three days after the surrender, it is as cold and chilling as November. Cooper sets the scene as a waste land. The mirror lake has been transformed by a howling wind so that "the green and angry waters lashed the shores, as if indignantly casting back its impurities to the polluted strand." These terms of infection, appearing alongside others suggesting the wrath of God, create a vision of hell. This is "a scene of wildness and desolation," where ravens feed off rotting corpses and where even the earth seems malignant, producing "dark green" tufts of grass which seem to have been "fattened with human blood" (p. 181).

In writing this description Cooper drew on Humphreys' *Life* of Israel Putnam, who had apparently visited the Fort the day after the Massacre. Yet there may be another, European source:

> Those poisonous fields with rank luxuriance crowned
> Where the dark scorpion gathers death around;
> Where at each step the stranger fears to wake
> The rattling terrors of the vengeful snake;
> Where crouching tigers wait their hapless prey,
> And savage men more murderous than they;
> While oft in whirls the mad tornado flies,
> Mingling the ravaged landschape with the skies.

Thus does Oliver Goldsmith depict America in *The Deserted Village*, written in the light of his reading about the French and Indian War for his *History of England*. *The Deserted Village* was published in 1770 and was immediately popular. It may well have prompted Dwight's image of Indians as "tigers in human form," and it had its effect on Cooper. Cooper knew too much about the flora and fauna of America to follow Goldsmith's errors, but the British writer's imagery of an environment that is storm-tossed, malevolent, and obscenely fecund seemed to find its appropriate locus on the shores of Lake George.[17]

I have suggested that *The Last of the Mohicans* reveals Cooper's indebtedness to such European writers as Montesquieu, Vattel, and Goldsmith, but it is far from being a derivative novel. Cooper was both a patriot and a sophisticated thinker, and the combination of these two attributes prompted him to bring European ideas firmly onto American terrain. The intellectual structure of the novel therefore follows the plot and spatial structures mentioned earlier. The Massacre at William Henry is a climax in the novel, but not its conclusion. Just as Cooper moves from the world of the whites to that of the Amerindians, so he tests European ideas by placing them in an alien environment. The result, I want to suggest, is a more enlightened view of Indian behavior and an attempt – although a muted and despairing one – to point out the lesson of the Massacre at Fort William Henry.

At first sight, Cooper seems to follow the excesses of Dwight in his attitudes to the Iroquois. Montcalm's allies, they commit the Massacre and he frequently calls them "savage." He also surrounds their leader, Magua, with diabolic images, most clearly when he refers to him as "the Prince of Darkness" (p. 284). This, however, is a quotation from *Paradise Lost,* and Milton depicted Satan as a magnificent figure, befitting his status as a fallen angel. Satan, once an inhabitant of heaven, had been expelled for breaking God's laws. Cooper depicts Magua similarly: as a superb warrior, a subtle speechmaker, and an effective and resourceful leader. His crime is that he breaks the white man's laws, starting the Massacre. He commits this crime, however, because a crime had been committed against him.

Early in Chapter 2 Duncan Heyward mentions a now-forgotten "idle tale" in which Magua was "rigidly dealt by" Colonel Munro (p. 21). The truth of the "idle tale" emerges when Magua is disputing the truce at William Henry with Montcalm. Munro beat Magua so severely for drunkenness that his back still bears the scars. After the surrender the French and the British act as "friends," but how can Magua be a friend after such humiliation? (p. 170)

Cooper gently reminds us of the significance of the humiliation by a series of six epigraphs drawn from *The Merchant of Venice,* one of them on the title page of the novel. Magua is thus not only Satan but also Shylock, seeking redress for a racial insult. Munro, otherwise presented as a gallant if old-fashioned soldier and a loving father, is in the position of Antonio, who is in Shylock's debt but spits on him and spurns him, calling him "misbeliever, cut-throat dog." It is a reflection on Heyward, too, that he should regard a racial insult as an "idle tale." Indeed, all three officers – Montcalm, Munro, and Heyward – try to practice their craft as if they are "on the fairest field of Europe." They make inadequate allowances for Indian attitudes.[18]

Vattel had said that no mercy should be given to savage nations who observed no rules. Cooper, who follows Vattel so closely in other respects, here parts company with him. The Indians have their own set of rules, and they observe them more punctiliously than the whites observe theirs. Cooper makes this clear in Chapters 30 and 31. The Delawares cannot detain Magua as he leaves their camp with the captive Cora Munro because of "the inviolable laws of Indian hospitality" (p. 317). With those words Chapter 30 ends. The epigraph for Chapter 31 is the one from *Henry V* that I quoted earlier. Agincourt may have been one of the fairest fields of Europe, a site of nostalgia for chivalrous soldiers like Montcalm, Munro, and Heyward, but it was also the site of broken laws. Cooper uses the epigraph for ironic purposes. He is attacking not just the French, but all whites. The Indians do not need a Grotius or a Vattel to teach them good behavior. They do not violate their law of arms.

Cooper underlines this point earlier in the novel, with the story of the "bloody pond." On September 6, 1755, British forces under Sir William Johnson defeated the French under Baron Dieskau at the Battle of Lake George. The next day, a British scouting party came upon a group of Canadians and Indians resting and eating by a pond. The surprise was complete, and the British filled the pond with the bodies of their enemies, dead and wounded alike. Significantly, Cooper goes into more detail about the atrocity than any of his known sources. In his version, furthermore, it is Natty Bumppo who leads the scouts, and whose motivation is revenge. The incident is a clear violation of the rules of Grotius and Vattel and the result, like the later Massacre at William Henry, is a pollution of the environment. The water of the pond, Natty remarks, was "coloured with blood, as natural water never yet flowed from the bowels of the 'arth." He adds that there isn't a square mile in the neighborhood he hasn't stained with the blood of an enemy or beast (pp. 135–6). Within the next page Chingachgook has added a French sentry to the corpses in the pond, but – and this is the vital point – as Natty remarks, the murder is allowable under Indian laws of war. Natty, however, is quite capable of committing what he calls "a cruel and an unhuman act for a white-skin" (p. 138). The frontiersman, too often treated by critics as one of nature's noblemen, is portrayed in *The Last of the Mohicans* as an adept and prolific killer. In this bloody novel, the earth is saturated with the blood that he has spilt.[19]

With the success of frontiersmen like Natty, the future looks bleak. Is *The Last of the Mohicans* also a meditation on the doom of America? Those majestic closing chapters might well lead us to think so. Yet I'd like to think that Cooper suggests, however tentatively, a means by which this "fatal region" may be redeemed. At first sight, the suggestion seems absurd. Cooper's antidote to the barbarity of the whites and the decline of the Indians is music. As we shall see, the antidote is in keeping with Cooper's Episcopalianism, and is suggested by Montesquieu. Early in *The Spirit of Laws,* Montesquieu speculates on the effect of music on the ancient Greeks. The "fierceness, indignation, and cruelty" for which they were famous had been inculcated by a regime of sports and military exercises. Music, says Montesquieu, can certainly excite similar emotions, but it can also "inspire the soul with a sense of pity, lenity, tenderness and love." He concludes that music is the most moral of the arts because "there is none that less corrupts the soul." He goes on to wonder about its effect in the wilderness:

> Let us suppose among ourselves a society of men so passionately fond of hunting as to make it their sole employment; they would doubtless contract a kind of rusticity and fierceness. But if they happen to imbibe a taste for music, we should quickly perceive a sensible difference in their customs and manners.[20]

This could be good news for America. It was certainly good news for musicians. In 1752 the English composer Charles Avison published *An Essay on Musical Expression*. He quoted Montesquieu at length and asserted that music had softened "the natural Rudeness and Barbarity of the *Arcadians.*" Only in one respect did he disagree with the French philosopher. Music cannot, he said, inspire "Hardheartedness, Anger, and Cruelty." He claimed, on the contrary, that martial music could "excite Courage and Contempt of Death, but never Hatred." Avison's book was popular. It went into a second edition the following year and was read, for instance, by Francis Hopkinson, the designer of the Stars and Stripes and the first composer to publish a book of music in America.[21]

Once again, Cooper tested a European idea in an American environment, and he did so by placing a psalm singer in *The Last of the Mohicans*. He signals the importance of the psalmodist by naming him David Gamut: Gamut because his voice is beautifully tuned to the musical scale, and David in honor of the first king of the Judean dynasty and the reputed author of the psalms. Will this American David conquer the Philistines as his namesake slew the heavily armored giant Goliath with a sling and a small stone? It seems unlikely, but the outcome is by no means a foregone conclusion, for he bears a powerful ideological burden. It has several components. In Christian teaching the biblical David was regarded as the type of Christ, although he was human and therefore sinful. His psalms were the model of the language of praise approved by God, and were sung as an expression of religious and family unity. They represented the epitome of the Christian struggle, and were frequently translated and often reprinted. A nineteenth-century authority lists 355 separate editions of the major English versions of the psalms by 1700, and a total of 1,134 by 1868.[22] Furthermore, the translation that Gamut uses is one of the most important early American cultural icons. *The Bay Psalm Book* first appeared in 1640; it was the first book printed in America. For about a century it was used all over New England and spread as far south as Philadelphia. Finally, Cooper presents his psalmodist as both a superb practitioner of his craft and a representative figure. It is likely, he says, "that no bard of profane song ever uttered notes that ascended so near to that throne, where all homage and praise is due." He was, moreover, "a minstrel of the western continent . . . after the spirit of his own age and country" (p. 118).

Yet Gamut, like the king for whom he is named, has a number of human imperfections. He is hardly a heroic figure. He is a very bad dresser. His body is out of proportion, with a large head, narrow shoulders, and long, gangling arms. His lower parts are even worse:

> His thighs and legs were thin nearly to emaciation, but of extraordinary length; and his knees would have been considered tremendous, had they not been outdone by the broader foundations on which this false superstructure of blended human orders, was so profanely reared. (p. 16)

This attempt at humor is, shall we say, a little heavy-footed. It does, however, leave us with a clear image of Gamut. The Bible tells us that King David "danced before the Lord with all his might." It is fortunate that his American namesake was not called on to follow suit. I doubt that the Lord would have been impressed.[23]

David Gamut's physical flaws are no doubt partly due to an Episcopalian New Yorker's dislike of New England Puritans. "Smart" Yankees are frequently found in Cooper's fiction and are rarely treated well. Gamut was not created purely out of prejudice, however. Cooper, I believe, wished to make a serious point about the psalmodist, and made that point by means of the text that Gamut uses. Cooper is very precise about this. Gamut has the highest praise for the text constantly by his side, the twenty-sixth edition of *The Bay Psalm Book;* published in 1744 (pp. 25–6), it had therefore been in circulation for thirteen years by the time of the action of the novel. In the 1740s, however, largely as a result of the Great Awakening, *The Bay Psalm Book* was falling out of favor. There was just one further edition, in 1762. The book was supplanted by the psalms and hymns of the English dissenter Isaac Watts. Watts's publications were enormously popular, but his references to the British monarchy made his *Psalms of David* unsuitable for post-Revolutionary America and republican versions were produced by Joel Barlow and Timothy Dwight. Dwight's was the better known, and it is likely that Cooper was familiar with it, for it was published in 1802, the year before Cooper went to Yale. There were several reasons why Cooper might prefer Watts to *The Bay Psalm Book*. Watts's theology was closer to Cooper's Episcopalianism and the translations of *The Bay Psalm Book* were notoriously ungainly. The meaning of the psalms was sometimes difficult to follow, and they were occasionally hard to sing. Watts's translations were less rigid, more elegant, and there was a closer consonance between words and music. If, therefore, the Montesquieu-Avison theory is correct, Watts would (in Congreve's words) "sooth the savage breast" more effectively than *The Bay Psalm Book.*[24] Gamut's devotion to it stacks the odds against him.

Gamut's human frailties and awkward psalm book are of a piece with Cooper's darkening vision of America. His singing can comfort his listeners, but it cannot solve the problems of the French and Indian War, as is made clear in one of the several episodes when David sings a psalm:

> The melody which no weakness could destroy, gradually wrought its sweet influence on the sense of those who heard it. It even prevailed over the miserable travesty of the Song of David, which the singer selected from a volume of similar effusions, and caused the sense to be forgotten, in the insinuating harmony of the sounds. Alice unconsciously dried her tears, and bent her melting eyes on the pallid features of Gamut, with an expression of chastened delight. . . . Cora bestowed an approving smile on the pious efforts of the namesake of the Jewish prince, and Heyward soon turned his steady, stern, look from the outlet of the cavern, to fasten it, with a milder character, on the face of David. . . . The open sympathy of the listeners stirred the spirit of the votary of music, whose voice regained its richness and volume, without losing that touching softness which proved its secret charm. (p. 84)

Cooper's distaste for *The Bay Psalm Book* is manifest, but the main point of the passage is the creation of an image of Christian unity. It also seems to prove that Montesquieu and Avison are right, because Heyward, who spends much of his time thinking about military glory, is softened by the song. But this fine set piece reaches its climax, and then collapses, within the next sentence:

> Exerting his renovated powers to their utmost, [David] was yet filling the arches of the cave with long and full tones, when a yell burst into the air without, that instantly stilled his pious strains, choking his voice suddenly, as though his heart had literally bounded into the passage of his throat. (p. 84)

Magua and his braves have found the cave at Glens Falls where the whites are hiding, and they rush into it, bellowing "cries and screams, such as man alone can utter, and he only when in a state of the fiercest barbarity" (p. 84).

The contrast could not be clearer: music, order, and softness on the one hand, and noise, disorder, and barbarity on the other.[25] Yet it would be going too far to conclude that this is the distinction between white and Indian worlds. Cooper's words are carefully chosen, and his closing phrases ("man alone" and "he only") indicate that his comments are not restricted to the Indians. For just as the Indians have their own law of arms, so they have their own music, and Cooper provides several examples of it. Late in the novel Uncas sings a war song, and when he is killed the Delaware women sing a song in his praise. It has a softening and unifying effect similar to that of David's psalm in the cave at Glens Falls:

> The Delawares themselves listened like charmed men; and it was very apparent, by the variations of their speaking countenances, how deep and true was their sympathy. Even David was not reluctant to lend his ears to the tones of voices so sweet; and long ere the chant was ended, his gaze announced that his soul was enthralled. (pp. 343–4)

This set piece does not collapse in disorder, however, and there is no hint of distaste. In the episode at Glens Falls, David's song had to rise above "the miserable travesty" of the Puritan words. In contrast, the Indians have music embedded into their language. When Uncas and Chingachgook talk together, the "melody" of their voices covers the complete gamut, "extending from the deepest bass to tones that were even feminine in softness" (p. 200). The Indians, it seems, are better musicians than the whites, just as they are better adherents to their law of arms.

The Indian laws of war and Indian music are unfortunately not consonant with those of the whites: During the Massacre at William Henry, Gamut starts singing a psalm, thinking that if King David could tame the evil spirit of Saul with sacred song, he should be able to tame the Indians. Gamut cannot stop the Massacre, but he and his companions are left unharmed. Indians rush up to them, bent on slaughter, but then pass on, "openly expressing their satisfaction at the firmness with which the white warrior sung his death song" (p. 177). This is a deeply black comedy of errors, indicating a conflict not between order and disorder, but rather between two different modes of order. We are now at the heart of the problem. For all their pluralism the European theorists were, inevitably and fatally, Eurocentric. The Montesquieu-Vattel laws of war and the Montesquieu-Avison theory of music were not framed to take account of the otherness of Indian civilization. Indian civilization is thus regarded as barbarism and the result is a holocaust. Magua is treated like Shylock and transformed into Satan. Insensitive to Indian civilization and motivated by greed, the whites draw down the inevitable retribution of death and destruction. America became, like many areas of the globe before and since, a fatal region. This was the lesson of the Massacre at Fort William Henry. It may be a lesson that we still have to learn.

NOTES

1. Jonathan Carver, *Three Years' Travels Throughout the Interior Parts of North America, in the Years 1766, 1767, and 1768* (1778; 4th American edition, Charlestown, Mass.: West and Greenleaf, 1802), 180–7. *The Pennsylvania Gazette* no. 1496 (August 25, 1757): 2 (original emphasis). The press report was first "Printed by Order" in the *New-York Mercury* of August 22, 1757, and reprinted, for instance, in *The London Magazine*, vol. 26 (1757): 494–5. Thomas Mante, *The History of the Late War in North-America* (London: W. Strahan and T. Cadell, 1772), p. 95. Jeremy Belknap, *The History of New Hampshire* (3 vols., Boston: Isaiah Thomas and Ebenezer Andrews, 1791), vol. 2, p. 299. Timothy Dwight, *Travels in New England and New York*, ed. Barbara Miller Solomon (first published 1822; 4 vols., Cambridge, Mass.: Belknap Press of Harvard University Press, 1969), vol. 3, p. 265. Francis Parkman, *Montcalm and Wolfe*, introd. Esmond Wright (first published 1884; London: Eyre and Spottiswoode, 1964), pp. 346–58. It is not certain that Carver witnessed the Massacre. A journal by the Colonel of the Massachusetts regiment, Joseph Frye, lists him as a captain, but omits the asterisk identifying those at Fort William Henry (Frye, "Fort William Henry," *Port Folio* 4th Ser., vol. 7, no. 5 [May 1819], p. 367). The veracity of other aspects of Carver's *Travels* was questioned shortly after its publication. See John Parker's "Introduction" to *The Journals of Jonathan Carver* (Minneapolis: Minnesota Historical Society

Press, 1976), and Robert Lawson-Peebles, *Landscape and Written Expression in Revolutionary America* (Cambridge, England: Cambridge University Press, 1988), p. 67.

2. Benjamin Trumbull, *A General History of the United States of America* (3 vols., Boston: Farrand, Mallory, & Co., 1810), vol. 1, pp. 372–3. David Humphreys, *An Essay on the Life of the Honourable Major General Israel Putnam* (1788; rpt. Boston: Samuel Avery, 1810), pp. 36–8. Discussions of Cooper's use of sources are to be found in David P. French, "James Fenimore Cooper and Fort William Henry," *American Literature*, vol. 32 (March 1960): 28–38; Thomas Philbrick, "The Sources of Cooper's Knowledge of Fort William Henry," *American Literature*, vol. 36 (May 1964): 209–16; Ian K. Steele, "Cooper and Clio: The Sources for 'A Narrative of 1757,'" *Canadian Review of American Studies*, vol. 20, no. 3 (Winter 1989): 121–35; and James Franklin Beard, "Historical Introduction" to *The Last of the Mohicans* (Albany: State University of New York Press, 1983), pp. xx–xxiv, xxx–xxxi.

3. Psalm 90:10, "The days of our years are threescore and ten." On the influence of Scott on Cooper, see George Dekker, *James Fenimore Cooper the Novelist* (London: Routledge and Kegan Paul, 1967) and Dekker, *The American Historical Romance* (Cambridge, England: Cambridge University Press, 1987).

4. For instance, the extended discussions with Lafayette reported in *Gleanings in Europe: The Rhine* (1836) are animated by Cooper's affection and respect for this relic of Franco-American Revolutionary amity, and make a strong contrast with his gloomy fears for the future of the United States. See James Franklin Beard, "Cooper and the Revolutionary Mythos," *Early American Literature*, vol. 11 (Spring 1976): 84–104, for a discussion of Cooper's emotional and imaginative involvement with the Revolutionary generation.

5. Andrew Delbanco, "Imagining America," *The New Republic* (June 9, 1986), p. 40.

6. On the structure of the novel, see John P. McWilliams, "Red Satan: Cooper and the American Indian Epic," *James Fenimore Cooper: New Critical Essays*, ed. Robert Clark (New York: Vision Press, 1985), p. 152; H. Daniel Peck, *A World by Itself: The Pastoral Moment in Cooper's Fiction* (New Haven: Yale University Press, 1977), pp. 109–45; and Donald Darnell, "Uncas as Hero: The *Ubi Sunt* Formula in *The Last of the Mohicans*," *American Literature*, vol. 37, no. 3 (November 1965): 259–66. On Cooper's synecdochal method, see John P. McWilliams, *Political Justice in a Republic: James Fenimore Cooper's America* (Berkeley:

University of California Press, 1972), pp. 11–12; and Robert Milder, *"The Last of the Mohicans* and the New World Fall," *American Literature,* vol. 52 (November 1980): 411.

7. Humphreys, *Israel Putnam,* p. 37. Mante, *History of the Late War,* p. 96. Tobias Smollett, *Continuation of the Complete History of England* (1760; rpt. 2 vols., London: Richard Baldwin, 1763), Vol. 1, p. 360; Vol. 2, pp. 42–3. Trumbull, *A General History,* Vol. 1, p. 373. Dwight, *Travels,* Vol. 3, pp. 265–6. Dwight describes the Oswego massacre in almost the same words as Smollett, but adds the phrase about "tigers in human shape." The most recent attack on Montcalm is to be found in Francis Jennings, *Empire of Fortune: Crowns, Colonies, and Tribes in the Seven Years War in America* (New York: W. W. Norton & Co., 1988), pp. 316–21. Jennings repeats Jonathan Carver's claim that the French denied the British any ammunition; but the soldiers may well have kept their bayonets, and the officers would certainly have retained their swords. The mass flight that troubled Mante, Smollett, and Trumbull still needs an explanation. It may well be provided by John Keegan's sensitive analysis of behavior under stress in *The Face of Battle: A Study of Agincourt, Waterloo and the Somme* (1976; rpt. Harmondsworth, Middlesex: Penguin, 1978). A detailed and balanced account of the incident, which came to hand too late to incorporate into my argument, is Ian K. Steele, *Betrayals: Fort William Henry and the "Massacre"* (New York: Oxford University Press, 1990).

8. *The Pennsylvania Gazette* no. 1496 (August 25, 1757): no. 2 (original emphasis); no. 1497 (September 1, 1757): 2. Smollett, *Continuation,* Vol. 2, p. 41. Mante, *History of the Late War,* p. 93. Frye, "Fort William Henry," p. 364.

9. Scott, *Guy Mannering* (1815; rpt. London: Adam and Charles Black, 1897), p. 289. Dryden, "Dedication to the Aeneis" (1697), in *Works,* ed. William Frost and Vinton A. Dearing (Berkeley: University of California Press, 1987), Vol. 5, p. 323.

10. Shakespeare does not see fit to explain Henry's order, given two lines earlier, to kill the French prisoners. *Henry V* IV.6.37, IV.7.1–3. For a discussion of Henry's decision, see Keegan, *The Face of Battle,* pp. 108–12. On the rules of combat, see M. H. Keen, *The Laws of War in the Late Middle Ages* (London: Routledge and Kegan Paul, 1965).

11. For brief details of the influence of Vattel in America, see Henry F. May, *The Enlightenment in America* (New York: Oxford University Press, 1976), pp. 89, 118; Gordon S. Wood, *The Creation of the American Republic, 1776–1787* (New York: W. W. Norton & Co., 1972), p. 355; and Brooks Mather Kelley, *Yale: A History* (New Haven: Yale

University Press, 1974), p. 109. A more detailed examination of Vattel's work is to be found in Stephen Ruddy, *International Law in the Enlightenment: The Background of Emmerich de Vattel's Le Droit des Gens* (Dobbs Ferry, New York: Oceana Publications, 1975).

12. Emmerich de Vattel, *The Law of Nations: Or, Principles of the Law of Nature* (first American edition, New York: Samuel Campbell, 1796), pp. 416–19, 481, 421.

13. Vattel, *The Law of Nations*, pp. xi, 371, 429, 422.

14. Charles de Secondat, Baron de Montesquieu, *The Spirit of Laws*, trans. Thomas Nugent, introd. Franz Neumann (2 vols. in 1, New York: Hafner, 1949), Vol. 1, pp. 5, 134. On the professionalization of the military, see Michael Howard, *War in European History* (Oxford: Oxford University Press, 1976), pp. 54–74. On fortifications, see Christopher Duffy, *The Fortress in the Age of Vauban and Frederick the Great 1660–1789* (London: Routledge and Kegan Paul, 1985), which, at pp. 71–2, talks briefly about Sébastien Le Prestre de Vauban (1633–1707).

15. Oliver Goldsmith, *The History of England from the Earliest Times to the Death of George II* (1771; rpt. 2 vols., London: John Harwood, 1824), Vol. 2, p. 404. On Cumberland, see W. A. Speck, *The Butcher: The Duke of Cumberland and the Suppression of the 45* (Oxford: Basil Blackwell, 1981), pp. 141–62.

16. Vattel, *The Law of Nations*, pp. 158–61, 416. Montesquieu, *The Spirit of Laws*, Vol. 1, p. 5. Goldsmith, *The History of England*, Vol. 2, p. 419.

17. Humphreys, *Israel Putnam*, p. 38. The relevant passage is reprinted in *The Last of the Mohicans*, pp. 363–4. Oliver Goldsmith, *The Deserted Village*, in *Collected Works*, ed. Arthur Friedman (6 vols., Oxford: Oxford University Press, 1966), Vol. 4, pp. 300–1.

18. Milton, *Paradise Lost*, Book 10, 1. 383. Shakespeare, *The Merchant of Venice*, I.3.108. John P. McWilliams' "The Historical Contexts" in the World's Classics edition of *The Last of the Mohicans* (Oxford: Oxford University Press, 1990), pp. 355–63, gives a good account of the complex Indian alliances, and comments on Cooper's use of the term "savage." Also see Milder, "*The Last of the Mohicans* and the New World Fall," and Joel Porte, *The Romance in America: Studies in Cooper, Poe, Hawthorne, Melville, and James* (Middletown, Conn.: Wesleyan University Press, 1969), pp. 22, 39–41.

19. Trumbull, *A General History*, Vol. 1, p. 355, gives a neutral account of "bloody pond," while Dwight's *Travels*, Vol. 3, p. 243, is somewhat more ominous. Wayne Franklin, *The New World of James Fenimore Cooper* (Chicago: University of Chicago Press, 1982), pp. 229–33,

gives a more detailed analysis of what he rightly calls "a devastatingly mortal terrain."

20. Montesquieu, *The Spirit of Laws,* Vol. 1, pp. 38–9.

21. Charles Avison, *An Essay on Musical Expression* (2d ed., London: C. Davis, 1753), pp. 12–19. The copy owned by Francis Hopkinson is held in the Rare Book Room of the Van Pelt Library, University of Pennsylvania.

22. Henry Alexander Glass, *The Story of the Psalters: A History of the Metrical Versions of Great Britain and America from 1549 to 1885* (London: Kegan Paul, Trench & Co., 1888), p. 10. Histories of psalmody in America are provided by Edward S. Ninde, *The Story of the American Hymn* (1921; rpt. New York: AMS Press, 1975), and Henry Wilder Foote, *Three Centuries of American Hymnody* (Cambridge, Mass.: Harvard University Press, 1940).

23. 2 Samuel 6:14. For a poignant view of Gamut as a disciple of order, see Franklin, *The New World of James Fenimore Cooper,* p. 248.

24. Isaac Watts, *The Psalms of David, Imitated in the Language of the New Testament, and adapted for Christian Use and Worship.* A New Edition . . . by Timothy Dwight, 1802 (rpt. New Haven, Conn.: Samuel Wadsworth, 1821). For a discussion of *The Bay Psalm Book,* see Norman S. Grabo, "How Bad is the Bay Psalm Book?" *Publications of the Michigan Academy of Science, Arts, and Letters,* Vol. 46 (1961): 605–14. William Congreve, *The Mourning Bride,* in *The Complete Plays,* ed. Herbert Davis (Chicago: University of Chicago Press, 1967), p. 326.

25. See Thomas Philbrick, "*The Last of the Mohicans* and the Sounds of Discord," *American Literature,* Vol. 43 (March 1971): 25–41.

Notes on Contributors

Nina Baym, Jubilee Professor of Liberal Arts and Sciences at the University of Illinois at Urbana-Champaign, is the author of *The Shape of Hawthorne's Career* (1976), *Women's Fiction: A Guide to Novels by and about Women in America, 1820–1870* (1978), *Novels, Readers, and Reviewers: Responses to Fiction in Antebellum America* (1984), and *The Scarlet Letter: A Reading* (1986).

Wayne Franklin, Professor of English and Director of American Studies at the University of Iowa, is the author of *Discoverers, Explorers, Settlers: The Diligent Writers of Early America* (1979) and *The New World of James Fenimore Cooper* (1982). His recent book, *A Rural Carpenter's World: The Craft in a Nineteenth-Century New York Township* (1990), appears in the American Land and Life Series of which he is general editor.

Robert Lawson-Peebles, Senior Lecturer in American and Commonwealth Arts at the University of Exeter, England, is the author of *Landscape and Written Expression in Revolutionary America* (1988) and co-editor of *Views of American Landscapes* (1989).

Terence Martin, Distinguished Professor of English at Indiana University, is the author of *The Instructed Vision: Scottish Common Sense Philosophy and the Origins of American Fiction* (1961) and *Nathaniel Hawthorne* (1964; rev. ed., 1983), and is a section editor of the *Columbia Literary History of the United States* (1988).

H. Daniel Peck, Professor of English and Director of the American Culture Program at Vassar College, is the author of *A World by Itself:*

The Pastoral Moment in Cooper's Fiction (1977) and *Thoreau's Morning Work: Memory and Perception in A Week on the Concord and Merrimack Rivers, the Journal, and Walden* (1990), and the editor of *The Green American Tradition: Essays and Poems for Sherman Paul* (1988).

Shirley Samuels, Assistant Professor of English at Cornell University, is currently completing a book entitled *Romances of the Republic: Politics and the Family in Antebellum America*, and is editor of *The Culture of Sentiment: Race, Gender, and Sentimentality in Nineteenth-Century America* (forthcoming 1992).

Selected Bibliography

All references to the text of *The Last of the Mohicans* in the foregoing essays are to the 1983 edition prepared for *The Writings of James Fenimore Cooper,* published by the State University of New York Press and edited by James Franklin Beard, James A. Sappenfield, and E. N. Feltskog.

Baym, Nina. "The Women of Cooper's Leatherstocking Tales." *American Quarterly* 23 (December 1971): 696–709.

Beard, James F. "Afterword" to *The Last of the Mohicans.* New York: New American Library, 1962.

"Historical Introduction," in *The Last of the Mohicans,* ed. Beard, James A. Sappenfield, and E. N. Feltskog. Albany: State University of New York Press, 1983.

Brownell, W. C. *American Prose Masters,* ed. Howard Mumford Jones. Cambridge, Mass.: Harvard University Press, 1967; first published in 1909 by Charles Scribner's Sons.

Butler, Michael D. "Narrative Structure and Historical Process in *The Last of the Mohicans.*" *American Literature* 48 (1976): 117–39.

Darnell, Donald. "Uncas as Hero: The *Ubi Sunt* Formula in *The Last of the Mohicans.*" *American Literature* 37 (November 1965): 259–66.

Dekker, George. *James Fenimore Cooper the Novelist.* London: Routledge and Kegan Paul, 1967.

Fiedler, Leslie. *Love and Death in the American Novel,* revised edition. New York: Dell Publishing Company, 1966.

Franklin, Wayne. *The New World of James Fenimore Cooper.* Chicago: University of Chicago Press, 1982.

French, David P. "James Fenimore Cooper and Fort William Henry." *American Literature* 32 (March 1960): 28–38.

Fussell, Edwin. *Frontier: American Literature and the American West.* Princeton: Princeton University Press, 1965.

House, Kay Seymour. *Cooper's Americans.* Columbus: Ohio State University Press, 1965.

Grossman, James. *James Fenimore Cooper.* Stanford: Stanford University Press, 1949.

Kelly, William P. *Plotting America's Past: Fenimore Cooper and the Leatherstocking Tales.* Carbondale, Ill.: Southern Illinois University Press, 1983.

Kolodny, Annette. *The Lay of the Land: Metaphor as Experience and History in American Life and Letters.* Chapel Hill: The University of North Carolina Press, 1975.

Lawrence, D. H. *Studies in Classic American Literature.* New York: The Viking Press, 1961; first published in 1923 by Thomas Seltzer.

Martin, Terence. "From the Ruins of History: *The Last of the Mohicans.*" *Novel: A Forum on Fiction* 2 (Spring 1969): 221–9.

McWilliams, John. "Introduction" and "The Historical Contexts of *The Last of the Mohicans,*" in *The Last of the Mohicans,* ed. McWilliams. New York: Oxford University Press, 1990.

   "'Red Satan': Cooper and the American Indian Epic," in *James Fenimore Cooper: New Critical Essays,* ed. Robert Clark. Totowa, N.J.: Barnes and Noble, 1985.

   Political Justice in a Republic: James Fenimore Cooper's America. Berkeley: University of California Press, 1972.

Milder, Robert. "*The Last of the Mohicans* and the New World Fall." *American Literature* 52 (November 1980): 407–29.

Nevius, Blake. *Cooper's Landscapes: An Essay on the Picturesque Vision.* Berkeley: University of California Press, 1976.

Pearce, Roy Harvey, "The Leatherstocking Tales Re-examined." *South Atlantic Quarterly* 46 (1947): 524–36.

Peck, H. Daniel. "James Fenimore Cooper and the Writers of the Frontier," in *The Columbia Literary History of the United States,* ed. Emory Elliott et al. New York: Columbia University Press, 1988.

   A World by Itself: The Pastoral Moment in Cooper's Fiction. New Haven: Yale University Press, 1977.

Philbrick, Thomas. "*The Last of the Mohicans* and the Sounds of Discord." *American Literature* 43 (March 1971): 25–41.

   "The Sources of Cooper's Knowledge of Fort William Henry." *American Literature* 36 (1964): 209–14.

Porte, Joel. *The Romance in America: Studies in Cooper, Poe, Hawthorne, Melville, and James.* Middletown, Conn.: Wesleyan University Press, 1969.

Railton, Stephen. *Fenimore Cooper: A Study of His Life and Imagination.* Princeton: Princeton University Press, 1978.

Ringe, Donald A. *James Fenimore Cooper.* New Haven: College and University Press, 1962.

   The Pictorial Mode: Space and Time in the Art of Bryant, Irving, and Cooper. Lexington: University of Kentucky Press, 1971.

Slotkin, Richard. *Regeneration through Violence: The Mythology of the American Frontier, 1600–1860*. Middletown, Conn.: Wesleyan University Press, 1973.

Smith, Henry Nash. *Virgin Land: The American West as Symbol and Myth.* Cambridge, Mass.: Harvard University Press, 1950.

Steele, Ian K. "Cooper and Clio: The Sources for 'A Narrative of 1757.' " *Canadian Review of American Studies* 20 (Winter 1989): 121–35.

Tompkins, Jane. "No Apologies for the Iroquois: A New Way to Read the Leatherstocking Novels," in her *Sensational Designs: The Cultural Work of American Fiction 1790–1860*. New York: Oxford University Press, 1985.